MUSIC SKILLS
for
RECREATION
LEADERS

BROWN

MUSIC SERIES

Edited by FREDERICK W. WESTPHAL, *Ph. D.*
Sacramento State College, Sacramento, California

MUSIC SKILLS

for

RECREATION LEADERS

FORREST J. BAIRD, Ed.D.

Professor, Music and Education

San Jose State College
San Jose, California

WM. C. BROWN COMPANY PUBLISHERS

135 SOUTH LOCUST STREET • DUBUQUE, IOWA

MT
87
.B3

Manufactured by WM. C. BROWN CO. INC., Dubuque, Iowa
Printed in U. S. A.

Foreword

The author has written *Music Skills for Recreation Leaders* drawn from the experience of several years of teaching Recreation Music as a course requirement for students enrolled in the recreation curriculum at San Jose State College. It is a comprehensive book that can be used by both the novice and the accomplished musician. One of the distinguishing features is its content coverage: singing activities, musical instruments for recreation, rhythmic activities and a section on listening to music.

The value of the book lies not only in the possibility of its use as a text for college courses, but in its use by volunteers or paid personnel in providing recreation services in hospitals, on military installations, in camps, with youth agencies, in municipal and industrial sponsored programs or within the pattern of family living.

As one of the cultural arts, music should be included as an integral part of a well planned recreation program. Participation in musical activities enables a group to quickly build an 'esprit de corps' and at the same time helps individuals to release inner tensions contributing to enriched living.

Dr. Mary S. Wiley
Head, Recreation Department
San Jose State College

Table of Contents

CHAPTER 1

Music and Recreation

What to do with all the free time available to them has become a major social problem for many people in this nation. Probably every one who reads this paragraph can remember a time when the working day for the average employed person was longer than it is today, and many of us have experienced the 70-hour week when a day off was a luxury that few could afford. Then came the 60-hour week, the ten hour day, and later the eight hour day; today the 40-hour week is more or less standard, but there is much talk about a 35-hour week. In most instances this reduction of hours on the job has been accomplished without an appreciable loss of income.

The marked decrease in the number of hours an individual is employed, and the resulting increase in the number of hours in which he has a free choice of activities, is presumed to lead to a more satisfying existence. This rises from the additional time available for relaxation, amusements, diversion, and recreation with a consequent recovery from the wear and tear that come from the stress and tensions of a work situation. Instead of the Utopian condition we had hoped for, however, there has been a growing problem of filling the interval of the day when the individual is not gainfully employed.

The years of early marriage and family rearing are generally considered optimum periods for home-centered recreational activities when the church, scouts, school, Parent Teachers Association, and similar social groups provide focal areas of interest for satisfying and enjoyable recreational activities for the entire family. As children mature and branch out on their own, the problem of leisure time becomes increasingly important for them and may become acute for their parents when they develop into senior citizens who retire from steady employment and break their regular work routines and patterns.

Overcrowded schools assume custody of a major portion of the youth population for six or seven hours daily on over half the days in the year, but what about the time when these young people are not in school? In *Youth Tell Their Story* Bell(1) cites "just loafing" as the predominant pastime or time killer for most of the young people surveyed. Up to 75 per cent of these individuals had no hobbies of a kind generally associated with youth.

McEntire's(2) study of a group of young people in Berkeley, California, indicated that youth from the lower socioeconomic levels generally do not participate in planned, organized recreational community activities; their activities are usually casual, unplanned, spur of the moment involvements that result from just walking, driving, or hanging around town. Together with increasing age comes a decline in park and playground activities, church attendance, movie going, and reading for most teen-agers.

Another critical situation develops when young people leave school. School-centered activities, associations, and social groupings break down. This break, coupled with a lack of saleable skills, low earning capacity, and failure of industry to absorb all young people who desire employment into the labor force, unite to cause unrest and insecurity in a large part of the population, especially those who do not continue their schooling into college.

Advanced education and college experience do not necessarily provide the answers to the challenges of free time. In *They Went to College,* a follow-up study of 951 former students at the University of Minnesota, Pace(3) wrote, "a balanced program (of college studies) should aim at a richer and more active life than is characteristic of these adults. Students should have more opportunities for inexpensive, creative activities and satisfying artistic experiences. Contributions of well-spent recreation time to satisfaction, adjustment, and family relationships should be continually emphasized."

Here let us summarize and review some of the elements that have created the persistent recreational problems at all age levels in our national population.

1. There has been an extremely rapid acceleration in the birth rate in the United States. Demographers had estimated a national population of 165 million by 1970, but by 1961 this figure had been surpassed by 20 million and our population was increasing at the rate of about 18,000 persons a month!

2. Medical science, improved nutrition, and better personal hygiene have increased individual life expectancy; consequently there are many older, non-working citizens with free time on their hands.

3. Compulsory education laws and higher educational requirements for entrance into preferred employment are postponing the time when young people can leave school and become self-sustaining members of our nation's work force.

These three factors produce the surprising fact that only 37 per cent of our total population, less than two out of every five persons in the United States, are gainfully employed; it is generally assumed that four or five million eligible persons will be temporarily or chronically unemployed in the country at any given time.

4. Large blocks of persons have moved from rural to urban areas with an inevitable reduction of play or recreation space in our cities. One hundred million of our total population in the United States live on one per cent of the nation's total land area.

5. Mechanization and automation have brought a general 40-hour, five-day week, and there is speculation on how long it will be before the 35-hour week is instituted.

6. The family unit no longer functions as a major work and recreational group. This may be an inescapable outcome of trends in urbanization and mechanization, but irrespective of the causes, a void which must be filled exists in the lives of many persons.

7. Conflicting ideas and traditions concerning work and leisure have been inherited from our past. Some of these were religious-centered and placed a high moral value on toil, "the sweat of the brow," or just plain busy work to keep one out of mischief. For example, in 1792 the discipline of the Methodist Church forbade "play in the strongest terms." These and similar concepts arose from the needs of a pioneer and frontier situation where men, women, and children worked from sunup to sundown to wrest the necessities of life from a wilderness. Even in these cultures the people, of necessity, gathered together to perform tasks that could not be accomplished by an individual or a family working alone. Round-ups; roof-raisings; threshing and slaughtering sessions; quilting and husking bees all were excuses for people to get together for work sessions. When the work was finished, the play and recreation began, providing refreshment, restoration, and diversion after physical work; when the dictates of the church would not allow square or folk dancing, these activities were called singing or play-party games.

Contemporary definitions interpret recreation as both an activity and an experience. The State of California Education Code(4) characterizes recreation as "any activity, voluntarily engaged in, which contributes to the physical, mental or moral development of the individual or group participating therein, and includes any activity in the fields of music, drama, art, handicraft, science, literature, nature study, nature contacting, aquatic sports, and athletics, or any of them, and any informal play incorporating any such activity."

The State of California Recreation Commission(5) has formulated and adopted another concept of recreation. "Recreation is an individual or a group experience motivated primarily by the pleasure derived therefrom. It takes many forms and may be a planned or a spontaneous activity. It is one of man's principal opportunities for enrichment of living and is the natural expression of certain human interests and needs."

These are broad and encompassing definitions that speak generally of a contribution to the "physical, mental or moral development" and of "man's principal opportunities for enrichment of living." There seems to be a need for more emphasis and care in these vital aspects of living, and in their book *Leisure and Recreation*, Neumeyer and Neumeyer(6) suggest these standards for evaluating leisure time activities:

1. The activity should be permanently interesting.
2. The activity should differ from the activities which the necessities of life impose upon the individual.
3. The activity should have its origin and fulfillment in the personality of the individual himself.
4. The activity should be compatible with, if not conducive to, the enrichment of life.

Some additional facts that should be considered are:

1. How much does it cost to participate in this activity? Will the satisfactions outweigh the cost involved?
2. Are facilities and equipment for this activity available in the community; can they be borrowed, rented, shared, or must the individual supply them for himself?
3. Is satisfactory instruction or coaching for this activity available in the community; can it be self-taught, or must one provide for his own concentrated, costly instruction?
4. Does this activity require regular, concentrated allotments of time, or can it be picked up and dropped without too much loss of facility?

Those of us who work with music believe that a strong interest or hobby in music can make a great contribution to the life of practically any individual, for music provides a satisfying outlet for creators, performers, or consumers. Music can utilize skills in building, in crafts, in collecting, or in research; it can involve one person at a time, or it may involve great hosts of people in a single musical venture; it may bring to bear a very high or a very limited talent or skill.

All of these music activities are interwoven and interdependent, but they can be grouped into the general areas or headings of singing, playing instruments, participating in rhythmic movements, or listening to music. Acquisition of information, vocabulary, and skills in these four areas of music can lead to membership in interesting groups in a variety of situations, for a common interest and a common purpose can open doors for new associations and new friendships. Then, too, much satisfaction can come from developing the ability to do something well.

Other outcomes or objectives of recreational music most generally mentioned are:

1. Music provides a wholesome and satisfying means of self-expression and self-realization.

For most of us these terms suggest the moulding of friendships; the feeling of belonging in a group or in an activity; the gaining of status within our group; the winning of social recognition, and the feeling of accomplishment for participation in activities that have value and significance in our social group.

2. Music enhances the cultural and esthetic life of the individual and develops in him an appreciation for music.

To appreciate music one must know the value or worth of musical experiences and be aware of the contribution that music can make to his life. Appreciation implies enough experience and exposure to music to enable the individual to make value judgments about this art form and to become a discriminating consumer or producer of music in his cultural situation.

Musical experiences make contributions to the development of individuals in these specific areas:

1. Physical skills

    Muscular coordination, the ability to reproduce musical patterns, the development of a physical, rhythmic response to music, and the use of the voice as a musical instrument.

2. Mental abilities

    The ability to concentrate on one subject area and to increase one's attention span.

3. Creative capacities

Use of imagination in creating responses to music, in the interpretation and re-creation of musical scores, or in creating new music.

4. Social development

Participants develop social courtesy by learning to take and follow instructions, knowing when and when not to be an active participant, taking turns, sharing experiences, and developing a feeling of responsibility for the success of a joint undertaking.

5. Information

Skill in finding, evaluating, and using information about music for itself and for its contribution in the four areas listed.

Studies indicate that public interest and demand are far ahead of offerings and opportunities in recreational music. In McEntire's investigation at Berkeley, California, mentioned earlier, persons polled rated the playing of a musical instrument as the most desired of recreational activities, but this was tenth among the activities actually participated in or available to them. In Isle's(7) *Stanford University Follow-up Inquiry*, listening to music, or so-called music appreciation courses, was rated third in a list of 27 general education courses most desired by Stanford graduates who participated in the study. A 1953-1954 survey of "Recreational Services in California School Districts" by C. Carson Conrad(8) indicates that of the 404 California school districts reporting, only 140 offered recreational music.

While these studies polled only a small segment of the total population in only one state, they indicate a strong demand for enlightened leadership in the development of a broadened program of recreational music for more people at all age and interest levels. This strong interest and demand might well be duplicated in other groups of people throughout the United States. Instrumental, reproduction equipment, and record sales would indicate that many persons are interested enough to do some trial and error experimentation.

Consider the potentialities for use of music in recreation centers, in camps, in hospitals, in penal institutions, in factories, in religious organizations, and in community centers. The selection of activities; provision for an adequate budget; and securing of facilities and leadership to meet the needs, wishes, and abilities of those who will become participants and consumers in the recreational music program call for careful thought and planning. Those responsible for this planning must consider (a) their own philosophies, attitudes, and values in this vital recreation area; (b) musical resources available in the community;

and (c) additional facilities, equipment, and leadership required to carry on a successful program.

An interested and informed recreation leader can make a significant contribution to recreational music by providing:

1. A sympathetic, informed attitude toward music in his program. This includes an awareness of the appeal and the contribution that music can make to recreational life in his community.

2. Motivation for surveys of the community to learn where and how music can be used and of the leadership resources, skills, and interest available in the situation.

3. Financial support to provide adequate facilities, equipment, and trained leadership for recreational music.

4. An organizational center to bring persons of like interests together as a vital step in the selection of appropriate activities. Joint planning and joint sponsorship of music activities can make for better utilization of community resources, possible standardization and sharing of costly equipment and facilities, and cooperation for in-service training programs. Perhaps the first step here would be the organization of a community date book or master calendar to avoid conflicting dates and duplication of services.

5. A clearing house or service center for records, films, and audio equipment. This could be operated in conjunction with schools, city or county libraries, or it could be handled independently as a recreational service. The function of getting the right equipment to the right place at the right time can be a vital and important matter in a music recreation program.

6. Files and listings of records, books, free materials, services, and equipment recommended or available to groups or individuals who care to use them.

7. Publicity for musical events in the community through news releases; bulletins and announcements; bulletin boards and posters featuring services, facilities, programs, and concerts that become available. Here again the community master calendar would be a helpful contribution.

8. For the development of his own leadership and performance skills in music.

In his *Fun Encyclopedia* E. O. Harbin(9) lists some musical skills that a recreation leader should acquire:

1. Ability to lead group singing
2. Ability to train a choir or chorus
3. Ability to train an orchestra

4. Ability to play a musical instrument
5. Experience in doing solo, duet, quartet, or chorus singing
6. Ability to arrange programs of music
7. Ability to recognize at least ten classical selections
8. Knowing at least twenty folk songs.

Kaplan(10), in *Music in Recreation,* expands Harbin's list with these items:

1. A wide knowledge of all types of songs
2. The know-how of making simple instruments
3. Ability to arrange music
4. Ability to put shows together.

As important and as desirable as each of these individual skills is, their absence should not prevent an interested recreation leader or administrator from making a strong and significant contribution to the utilization of music in his program. Equally important are his administrative abilities and his functions in choosing activities within the interests and skill ranges of his clients, providing trained and adequate personnel, utilizing available resources, recognizing and encouraging growth toward attainable goals, and fostering and enjoying participation in worthwhile and important music recreation.

The remaining chapters of this book are devoted to singing, playing instruments, rhythmic activities, and listening to music. The material presented should serve to indicate some avenues of approach, some available resources, and some situations in which music can be used in a recreation program. Remember that the success of your program is dependent upon your enthusiasm, your careful planning, your imagination, your hard work, and your patience as well as upon your abilities as a musician; you have the capacity to grow and to increase your skill in each of these areas.

REFERENCES

1. Howard Bell. *Youth Tell Their Story.* Washington, D. C.: American Council of Education, 1938.
2. Davis McEntire. "Leisure Activities of Youth in Berkeley, California," Berkeley Council of Social Welfare and the School of Social Welfare, University of California, Berkeley, California, 1952.
3. C. Robert Pace. *They Went to College.* Minneapolis: University of Minnesota Press, 1941.
4. California State Department of Education. *Education Code.* Sacramento: State Printing Office, 1953.

5. State of California Recreation Commission. *Recreation in California, Eighth Annual Report.* Sacramento, 1956.
6. W. H. Neumeyer and E. Neumeyer. *Leisure and Education.* New York: Barnes, 1936.
7. Walter W. Isle. "The Stanford University Follow-up Inquiry: A Study of Stanford's Teacher Preparation Services." Unpublished Ed. D. dissertation, Stanford University, 1942.
8. C. Carson Conrad. "Recreational Services in California School Districts," *California Schools*, March, 1960.
9. E. O. Harbin. *Fun Encyclopedia.* New York: Association Publishers, 1940.
10. Max Kaplan. *Music in Recreation.* Champaign, Illinois: Stipes Publishing Company, 1955.

TOPICS FOR DISCUSSION AND ASSIGNMENT
General

1. What contribution does music make to your personal recreational life?
2. Is music used for recreation in your home?
3. How do you participate in musical activities?
4. Make a list of your own musical skills.
5. As a recreation leader what musical skills would you like to have?
6. How can music be used in the recreational life of your community?
7. Develop a questionnaire that would discover the music resources and needs of your recreation clientele.
8. Build a file or scrapbook of music materials of value to you.
9. Organize a file of materials to be used for bulletin board displays to encourage musical activities.
10. Plan and create a bulletin board display to stimulate interest in community music projects.

CHAPTER 2

Singing

Singing activities are the easiest means of music participation available to large or small recreation groups of practically any age. Singers with little previous knowledge or experience in music can join in a formal or informal situation indoors or out to find satisfaction, emotional release, and entertainment for themselves and others about them. Singing is conducive to group formation; through song the individual identifies himself with other persons, places, and things. Participation in group singing brings feelings of belongingness, fosters group spirit, and builds morale. There is no audience; everyone performs, and the bashful soon forget themselves.

THE SONGLEADER'S FUNCTIONS

If the group is to gain satisfaction from its singing activities, the song leader must know and use the full vocal resources of the participants. In an informal situation, grouping or seating arrangements may not be important so long as the singers are close together, but when special effects are to be worked for, group arrangement should be considered. Even in unison singing it is a good idea to put strong singers in the back or center of the group to lead out and give confidence to the weaker singers.

The function of the song leader varies with the size and formation of the singing ensemble. Musical knowledge and musical perfection are of secondary importance in many recreational situations, but irrespective of the situation, the director must do enough preplanning and preparation to (1) be at ease before his group; (2) have a well-planned and varied sequence of songs; (3) know his songs; (4) inform the group of what they are to do; (5) make the session enjoyable for the participants; and above all else, (6) know when to stop! Remember that a well-planned program is the best start toward a successful session. It is good procedure to start with a simple, familiar song well-known to the singers, then move easily from one song to the next without too much loss of time.

Before starting a song, the leader must know its key, range, and starting tone; he must be aware of meter, mood, and tempo which come directly from the text of the song. Some of these can be established by a strong musical introduction played on an accompanying instrument. If no accompanying instrument is available, the song director can use a pitch pipe. After setting the pitch, the leader must, at least mentally, establish the key center (1 − 3 − 5, doh − mi − sol) and the starting tone. This he must communicate to his singers. When the song is to be done in unison, one pitch is all that is needed, but if the song is to be done in parts, pitches for the other voices must be established. The key establishes the range in which the song is to be sung. For general, comfortable singing by mixed groups, songs should not go above D or Eb in the staff or much below middle C.

The leader has several methods whereby he can communicate his ideas to the musicians. They can learn their interpretation of the music by rote, by imitation of the leader, or from a good recording. The leader may talk the group into a musical interpretation of a song, or he may be an expressive enough conductor that, through his motions, gestures, and facial expressions, he can communicate his feelings to the singers. In an informal situation it may be that the leader will not think it necessary to conduct formally or throughout the entire song. He should at least get the singers started at the same time and give them a model for tempo, dynamics, and phrasing.

CONDUCTING

A trained recreation director should know and be able to use formal conducting patterns if the need arises. When used correctly these patterns bring the singers to attention, start the group simultaneously, indicate the regular tempo of the music as well as any variations, the meter, accents, dynamics, and finally the termination of the musical selection.

Beat patterns are standardized and generally known. Until the pattern can be maintained without conscious effort, it is suggested that the beginning conductor practice before a full-length mirror.

Before he starts to conduct, his hands should be held in such a position that they, with the face, form a triangle. This position is maintained until the attention of every member of the group is secured.

In music that has two beats or pulses to a measure such as 2-4, 2-2, or a fast 6-8, the right hand motion is down, up; down, up; first count on the down beat and second count on the up beat.

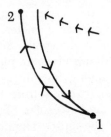

The broken line indicates the preparatory beat which must be given clearly as preparation before the beat of execution or the signal to start singing. It is used in all meters and tempos and indicates the speed of the music to follow. In singing or in playing wind instruments, this is the time when the performers take their breath for the initial attack. The first beat in every measure, irrespective of the meter, is a down beat, and the beat before the down beat is usually upward and from the director's right side.

Practice these songs in 2-4 meter:

ARE YOU SLEEPING?

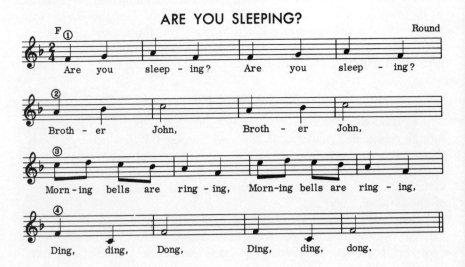

YANKEE DOODLE

Traditional

Fa-ther and I went down to camp a - long with Cap-tain Good-in, And there we saw the men and boys as thick as has -ty pud - ding;

Yan -kee doo -dle, keep it up, Yan-kee doo-dle dan - dy, Mind the mu-sic and the step and with the girls be han - dy.

WHERE, OH, WHERE?

Student Song

Where, oh, where are the ver - dant Fresh - men? Where, oh,
gay young, Soph - mores?
where are the ver - dant Fresh- men? Where, oh, where are the
ver - dant Fresh-men? Safe now in the Soph'more class.
Jun - ior

CARRY ME BACK TO OLD VIRGINNY

Bland

Car -ry me back to old Vir - gin - ny
There's where the cot -ton and the corn and 'ta - ters grow,
There's where the birds war -ble sweet in the spring-time,
There's where this old heart of mine does long to go.

13

DIXIE

Wish I was in the land of cot - ton, old times there are not for-got-ten, look a - way, look a - way, look a - way Dix - ie land.

In music that has three beats or pulses to a measure, such as 3-4, 3-8, 3-2, or a fast 9-8, the right hand motion is down, right, up; down, right, up; and the first count of each measure is on the down beat, second count to the right, and the third count on the up beat.

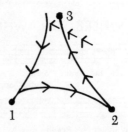

Notice that the preparatory beat is given from the leader's right side, that the down beat curves slightly to the left, and that the last beat in the measure comes up from the right side. The curved down beat takes some of the weight from the hand and makes for a more graceful, flowing motion than a straight down beat.

AMERICA

Carey

My coun - try, 'tis of thee, Sweet land of lib - er - ty, Of thee I sing. Land where my fa - thers died. Land of the Pil-grim's pride. From ev - 'ry moun - tain side, Let free - dom ring!

FAITH OF OUR FATHERS

COME, THOU ALMIGHTY KING

In a very fast three meter where this triangular beat would be clumsy or cumbersome, it is permissible to direct just one beat to a measure similar to beat used in two pulse measures.

SIDEWALKS OF NEW YORK

In music that has four beats or pulses to a measure such as 4-4, 4-8, 4-2, or a fast 12-8, there is a combination of two, two groupings. The right hand motion is down, left, right, up; down, left, right, up; first count on the down beat, second count to the left, third count to the right, and fourth count on the up beat.

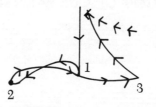

Again, the preparatory beat is given from the leader's right side. Four-four meter can be indicated by a large letter C after the key signature. So many of our well-known songs are in a four beat meter that the large C is referred to as "Common Time."

LONG, LONG AGO

Tell me the tales that to me were so dear, Long, long a-go, long, long a-go.

Sing me the songs I de-light-ed to hear, Long, long, a-go, long a-go;

Now you are come, all my grief is re-moved, Let me for-get that so long you have roved.

Let me be-lieve that you love as you loved, Long, long a-go, long a-go.

CRUSADERS' HYMN

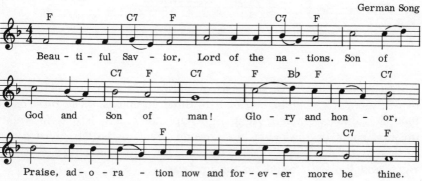

Beau - ti - ful Sav - ior, Lord of the na - tions. Son of

God and Son of man! Glo - ry and hon - or,

Praise, ad - o - ra - tion now and for - ev - er more be thine.

GOD OF OUR FATHERS

Warren

God of our fa - thers, whose al - might - y hand,

Leads forth in beau - ty all the star - ry band

of shin - ing worlds in splen - dor thru the skies,

Our grate - ful songs be - fore Thy throne a - rise.

HOLY, HOLY, HOLY

Dykes

Ho - ly, ho - ly, ho - ly, Lord God Al - might - y! Ear - ly in the

morn - ing our song shall rise to Thee; Ho - ly, ho - ly, ho - ly!

Mer - ci - ful and might - y! Who wert, and art, and ev - er - more shall be.

In meters that have six beats or pulses to a measure such as 6-8 or 6-4, there is a combination of two, three groupings. The right hand motion is down, left, left, right, right, up; down, left, left, right, right, up; first count on the down beat, second count to the left, third count farther to the left, fourth count to the right, fifth count farther to the right, and the sixth count on the up beat.

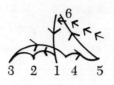

or

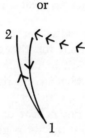

SILENT NIGHT

In a fast six meter where it would be difficult to execute or follow the six beat pattern, it is customary to beat just two beats in a measure and to group three pulses or their equivalent on the down beat and three pulses on the up beat.

LAZY MARY WILL YOU GET UP?

It is permissible in any situation to beat a measure or two in rhythm before giving the signal for the group to sing. In four-four meter the director may beat out a measure and say, "One, two, ready, sing," and the group would start on the first or down beat of the next measure.

Not all songs start on a down beat or on the accented part of the measure. "America, the Beautiful" is a good example.

AMERICA, THE BEAUTIFUL

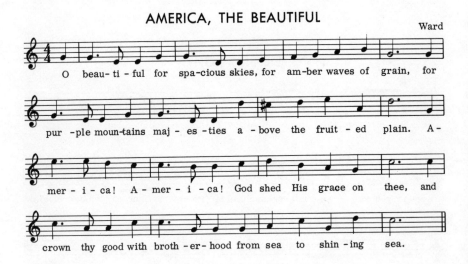

Here the primary accent doesn't fall on the first word but on the second word. One would not sing

1   2 3 4 1   2   3   4
"O beautiful for spacious skies" but

4   1 2 3 4   1   2   3
"O beautiful for spacious skies"

and in this case the value of the first or pickup beat is subtracted from the final measure of the song. The preparatory beat would now be given from left to right:

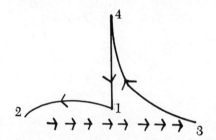

If this seems difficult or does not give a smooth start, try beating a full measure and saying "One, ready, sing, 'O'," starting to sing on the fourth beat of the measure. In a three meter one would start to beat and say, "Ready, sing, 'O'," as the singing starts on the third beat of the measure.

It is desirable to finish a song with the hands in a position of rest and repose. For example, take the last two measures of "America." One would beat:

"Let freedom ring"
1   2 3 1 2 3

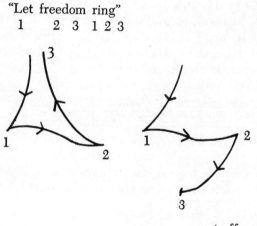

cut-off and stop.

On the final beat, one might use both hands to form the shape of a bowl. This brings the number to a close with the hands in a natural rest position, about waist high.

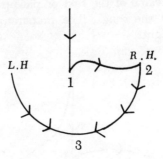

When the cut-off occurs on the second beat of a three pulse measure, the pattern will look like this:

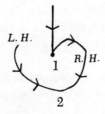

Fermatas or holds, indicated by a ⌢ , may occur on any beat of any measure. When this sign occurs, the regular pulsation or re-occurring beat stops for as long as the director cares to sustain the note so indicated. If there is no director, the general rule is to increase the value of the note by one-half its original value. In "Long, Long Ago" the notation is sometimes indicated:

Long, long a - go,   long   a - go.

This would be beat in the regular fashion but with a hold on the first half of the fourth beat. The beat pattern would be:

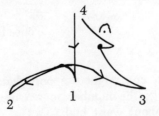

The director would hold as long as he wishes, proceed with the remainder of his fourth beat, and on to the next measure. No cut-off or new start is needed as a part of the fourth beat; the signal to go on is the signal to terminate the hold, catch a breath, and move on!

The right hand and arm are of primary importance in conducting; they indicate the meter and tempo of the song. The right hand may also indicate dynamic levels by the size or elevation of the beat, a small, low beat indicating a low dynamic level, a large, high beat indicating a high dynamic level. The left hand is used to emphasize accents, to support and strengthen the dynamic levels suggested by the right hand, and to give special group or sectional cues. Above all else, use the left hand sparingly. It doesn't have to tag along with the right hand all the time.

SONG INTRODUCTIONS

It was mentioned earlier in this chapter that a good introduction, played by a skilled accompanist, should indicate the tempo, tonality, and mood of the song to follow. When playing for an inexperienced group of singers, the accompanist should end the introduction on the pitch with which the singers are to start; experienced singers will have little trouble finding their starting pitch in the final chord of the introduction.

Introductions may be played on an accompanying instrument or sung by the director. The length of the introduction may vary with the length and familiarity of the song being used. In general, the last four or eight measures of the song, or the first four measures of the song followed by the last four measures, will suffice. If the song is short or if it is a new song, it may help to play or sing one stanza all the way through as an introduction.

TEACHING NEW SONGS

There are three accepted methods of teaching a song by ear or by rote:

1. the part method,
2. the whole method,
3. the phrase method.

In the part method the group is invited to join in on a section of the song which is repeated at regular intervals. "Go Down Moses," "Swing Low Sweet Chariot," and "Old MacDonald Had a Farm" are examples of songs that could be taught in this manner. For instance, after a group has heard "Swing Low" several times, this routine could be tried.

Leader: SWING LOW, SWEET CHARIOT,

Group: COMIN' FOR TO CARRY ME HOME,

Leader: SWING LOW, SWEET CHARIOT,

Group: COMIN' FOR TO CARRY ME HOME.

Leader: I LOOKED OVER JORDAN, AND WHAT DID I SEE,

Group: COMIN' FOR TO CARRY ME HOME?

Leader: A BAND OF ANGELS, COMIN' AFTER ME,

Group: COMIN' FOR TO CARRY ME HOME.

Next, individual singers could join the leader in any parts of the song they remembered, and finally, the group should sing the song without help from the leader.

The whole method teaches the complete song or stanza by exposure and repetition until the group can sing it in its entirety. One proof of the effectiveness of this system is the ease with which people learn songs by hearing them from radio or television broadcasts. The leader can sing the song for the group, have the song presented by an individual or by a small ensemble from the group, or use a recording to familiarize his singers with the new song. After several repetitions of the song on several days, and depending upon the interest shown by the group, the singers are invited to join in the fun. If there are sections or phrases that need correction, these should be isolated and rehearsed until satisfactory results are achieved.

The phrase method starts with presentation of the entire song by the leader; he then sings the first phrase of the song and the group sings it back to him. He sings the second phrase of the song, and the group sings it back to him. This procedure is repeated until the stanza or stanzas are learned. For instance, in "Bobby Shafto" the leader would sing the first two measures of the song, and the group would sing the same two measures on the repeat. This procedure would be continued on through the song until the group could sing the entire song from memory.

BOBBY SHAFTO

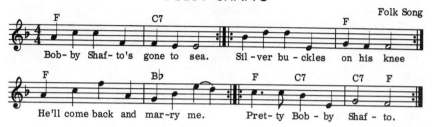

In these learning processes there will be songs at various levels. Some songs will be at the "familiarizing" stage, some at the "working out" stage, and some at the "polishing" or "enrichment" stage. The songs in the "working out" stage should be placed early in the song session, just after the "warm-up" period, when group attention and interest are at their best.

IMPROVEMENT OF GROUP SINGING

Enjoyment is the first and greatest objective in all recreation music activities. Musically speaking the leader must start where he finds his group, but he and they should not be satisfied to stay there. The goals for a vocal group include:

1. Accurate pitch and rhythm in all parts. The rhythm of the text usually dictates the musical notation used; sometimes it is helpful to say the words of a song in rhythm before trying to sing them.

2. Feeling for dynamic and rhythmic phrases. These also are dictated by the text of the song; try to tell a story as you sing. Find the important words or concepts in each phrase and build towards them. Generally the group will breathe at punctuation marks, at the end of long tones, or after some consonant sounds at the ends of words. Breathing at the right places will help to build a feeling for phrases.

3. Uniform concept of tone and vowel sounds throughout the group. There are only five fundamental vowel sounds — ah, a, e, o, oo — used in singing. The secret is to find the underlying vowel sound in each syllable or word and to sustain and purify it as much as possible. Consonants give meaning to the vowel sounds; they must be clearly enunciated by the correct use of tongue, teeth, and lips. All of this contributes

to an expressive text combined with the expressiveness of the melody. Following is an analysis of the underlying vowel sounds in a well-known song:

Now	the	day	is	over
ah-oo	ah	a	e	o ah

Night	is	drawing	nigh
ah-e	e	ah e	ah-e

Shadows	of	the	evening
ah o	ah	e	e e

Steal	across	the	sky.
e	ah ah	ah	ah-e

Notice that "the" before the vowel in "evening" has a long "e" sound, while "the" before the consonant in "sky" has an "ah" sound.

4. Precise attacks and releases of pitches in all voices. Have the singers breathe together on the preparatory beat before they start to sing. Sometimes it helps to put an "h" before a vowel to avoid a stuttering effect on a soft, initial attack.

SONG ENRICHMENT

It is a good idea to finish the song session with familiar material to be "polished" or "enriched." A typical song session might include a song sequence in this order:

1. Songs well-known to the group
2. Working out parts of a song that is new to the group
3. Enrichment of a familiar song
4. Solo or small group presenting a new song
5. Familiar songs which could be requested by the group.

Above all, finish while the interest is still high. Leave them while they still want more!

There are numerous ways to achieve variety and enrichment even when only the melodic line of the song is used. Try some of these:

1. Whistle the tune.
2. Hum the melody.
   To achieve good results in humming, press the lips together, place the tip of the tongue against the upper teeth, and think

"hm" while vocalizing. For a louder sound, keep the lips parted, tongue against the upper teeth, and think "hn" while vocalizing.

3. Clap and combine the rhythms of the song.
   Divide the group into sections and have one section clap on the first beat of the measure, another on each beat of the measure, and still another clap the rhythm of the melody. Achieve different sounds by clapping on different parts of the hands or by tapping on various surfaces such as wood, metals, plastics, etc.

4. Draw the rhythm of the beat with your hand or arm.
   This can be done in the air or on a surface. For example:

3-4

4-4

5. Have all the group conduct the song along with the leader.
6. Draw the melodic line in terms of duration and pitch, high or low.

> *Mer-ri-ly,*
>   *mer-ri-ly,*   *life*
>   *mer-ri-ly,* *is* *but* *a*
>   *mer-ri-ly*   *dream*

This, too, can be done in the air or on a surface.

7. Recite the words as in choral speaking, contrasting high and low voices.
   Be sure to discuss the story that is being told.
8. Tell the group the story of the song, its national background, about its composer, or how it happened to be written.

9. Contrast solo and group singing. Try "Swing Low," "Go Down, Moses," "The Deacon Went Down," "Sweet Adeline," and "Vive L'amour" this way or with competing groups.

GO DOWN MOSES

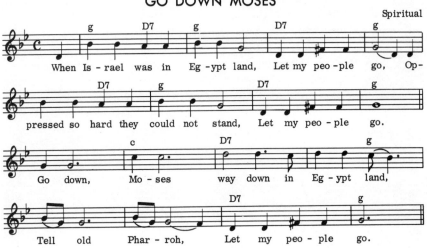

VIVE L'AMOUR

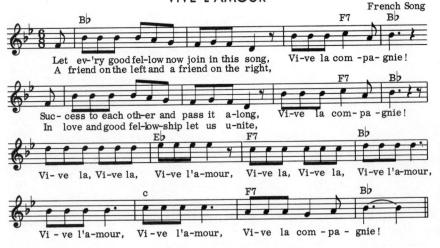

Cumulative songs such as "The Orchestra," "The Twelve Days of Christmas," and "Alouette" also can be used this way.

THE ORCHESTRA

10. Use some nonsense songs or parodies. "Ta-ra-ra-boom-de-ay," "Chum-ba-ra," or "Boola-boola" can be sung using just those words.

BOOLA-BOOLA

College Song

CHUM-BA-RA, CHUM-BARA

Folk Song

1. Chumbara
2. Fiddolee
3. Trumpetor

c b c b c b c b   c b c

c = Chum, b = ba

TA-RA-RA BOOM-DE-AY

Sagers

TO-ROO-LAY

Folk Melody

"Dark Eyes," "Chapanecas," or "The Jolly Coppersmith" can be done with "lah."

DARK EYES (LAH)

Russian Song

CHAPANECAS (LAH)

Mexican

JOLLY COPPERSMITH (LAH)

Peter

11. Use contra singing, in which two songs are sung at the same time; this is difficult to do, but it is fun if the group is capable. Be sure that one tune is well established before the second is introduced. Songs that fit together include:
    a. Most rounds

SWEETLY SINGS THE DONKEY and WHERE IS JOHN?
(Combined)

Rounds

Sweet-ly sings the don - key   at   the   break   of   day;

Where   is   John?   The   old   grey   hen   has   left   her   pen;

If   you   do   not   feed   him,   this   is   what he'll   say: Hee -

Where   is   John?   The   cows   are   in   the   corn a-gain, Oh,

haw,   Hee - haw,   Hee - haw, Hee-haw, Hee -haw!

John!

b.   "Oh, Where Has My Dog Gone?" and "Tippi-Tippi-Tin"

WHERE, OH WHERE, and TIPPI-TIPPI-TIN
(Combined)

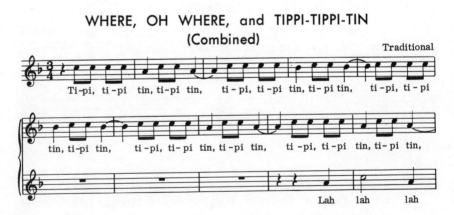

Traditional

Ti-pi, ti -pi tin, ti-pi tin,   ti - pi, ti -pi tin, ti- pi tin,   ti-pi, ti -pi

tin, ti-pi tin,   ti -pi, ti -pi tin, ti -pi tin,   ti - pi, ti -pi tin, ti- pi tin,

Lah   lah   lah

c. "Spanish Cavalier" and "Solomon Levi"

SPANISH CAVALIER and SOLOMON LEVI
(Combined)

Hendrickson
Traditional

Oh, say dar - ling say, when I'm far a - way,

Some times you may think of me, dear;

Bright sun - ny days will soon fade a - way, Re - mem - ber what I say and be true dear.

d. "Rocka My Soul" and "Ten Little Indians"

ROCKA MY SOUL and TEN LITTLE INDIANS
(Combined)

Spiritual
Traditional

One lit-tle, two lit-tle, three lit-tle In - dians; four lit-tle, five lit-tle, six lit-tle In - dians; seven lit-tle, eight lit-tle, nine lit - tle In - dians; ten lit-tle In - dian boys.

Rock my soul in the bos-om of A - bra-ham Rock my soul in the bos-om of A-bra-ham Rock my soul in the bos-om of A-bra-ham Oh! Rock-a my soul.

e. "There's a Long, Long Trail" and "Keep the Home Fires Burning" are given in part. Try to complete them.

THERE'S A LONG, LONG TRAIL and
KEEP THE HOME FIRES BURNING
(Combined)

There's a   long, long trail a' wind-ing   in-to the   land of   my

Keep   the home fires burn - ing   while your hearts are

f. "Swanee River" and "Humoresque" (Key of C)

g. "Tipperary" and "Pack Up Your Troubles" (Key of C)

12. Act out the story in the song. Suggested songs are:

 a. "There Was a Crooked Man"

 b. "Eency, Weency Spider"

 c. "Jack and Jill"

 d. "Speak Louder"

 e. "Hole in the Bucket"

13. Sing songs in foreign languages.

 a. French

ALOUETTE

French

A - lou-et-te, gen-tile A-lou-et-te,   A - lou-et -te, Je te plu-me-rai.

1. Je te plu- me-rai la tete, Je te plu-me-rai la tete, Et la tete, *(Again)* Oh!
2. Je te plu- me-rai le bec, Je te plu-me-rai le bec, Et la bec,
3. Le nez; 4. Le dos; 5. Les pattes; 6. Le cou

b. Spanish and Mexican

EL CHARRO

c. Latin

DONA NOBIS PACEM

Do - nna no - bis pa - cem, pa-cem, do -nna no - bis pa - cem.

Do - nna no - bis pa -cem, do-nna no -bis pa - cem.

Do - nna no - bis pa - cem, do -nna no - bis pa - cem.

O COME, ALL YE FAITHFUL (ADESTE FIDELIS)

O come, all ye faith - ful, joy - ful and tri - um-phant; O
A - des - te fi - de - lis, lae - ti tri - um -phan - tes; Ve -

come ye, O come ye to Beth - le - hem;
ni - te, ve - ni - te in Beth - le - hem;

Come and be - hold Him born the King of an - gels; O
Na - tum vi - de - te, Re - gem an - ge - lo - rum, Ve -

come, let us a - dore Him, O come let us a - dore Him, O
ni - te, ad - o - re - mus, Ve - ni - te, ad - o - re - mus, Ve -

come, let us a - dore Him, Christ the Lord.
ni - te, ad - or - re - mus, Do - mi - num.

d. German

DU, DU, LIEGST MIR IM HERZEN

Folk Song

Du, du leigst mir im Her-zen, Du, du leigst mir im Sinn;

Du, du machst mir viel Schmer-zen weist nicht wie gut ich dir bin;

Ja, ja, ja, ja, weist nicht wie gut ich dir bin.

O DU LIEBER AUGUSTIN

Folk Song

O du lie-ber Au-gus-tin, Au-gus-tin, Au-gus-tin,

O du lie-ber Au-gus-tin, al-les ist hin!

Geld is weg, Mad'l is weg, al-les weg, al-les weg,

O du lie-ber Au-gus-tin, al-les ist hin!

e. Japanese

MINISAMA

Adapted

Mi-ni-sa-ma, mi-ni-sa-ma, i-ka-ga? i-ka-ga? Ar-i-ga-to,

gen-ki des'; ar-i-ga-to, gen-ki des'. I-ka-ga, an-at-a-wa?

JAPANESE GREETING SONG

Mo-shi, Mo-shi a - no ne, a-no ne, a-no ne. Mo-shi, mo-shi, a- no ne, A, so des ka. Ko -chi me te ku-da-sai, ku - da-sai, ku -da-sai. Ko - chi me te ku - da - sai, 'A - li - ga - to.

14. Sing a medley of songs using related keys but contrasting tempi and moods. These can be built around a central idea such as "through the day in song;" "by months for birthdays in the group;" "a trip across the country with recognition of states or nations;" "something old, something new, something borrowed, something blue;" or "holidays." Medleys often may evolve from the requests by members of the singing group once a varied repertory has been developed.

HARMONIZATION OR PART SINGING

Singing of parts or vocal harmonizing opens another large resource area. The parts can be introduced formally or informally. Many times the more experienced singers in the group will fall very naturally into a harmony part while singing a familiar song. Often the strong singers are placed in the center of the group so they can lead the way in harmonizing.

The quickest and easiest way to accustom singers to hear parts other than the melodic line is through the introduction of an accompaniment. This builds an awareness of something else going on along with the melody.

Another approach to part singing is to sing rounds and canons. A round is defined as a composition in which the voices sing the same music, but the starting voices sing a complete musical phrase before the second voices and succeeding voices enter. Rounds can be sung in unison or in series, but at the beginning stage it may be advantageous to sing the round in unison. After the tune is learned, each voice or group of voices should sing the melody through a prede-

termined number of times and end singly. This is known as series
singing.

(*SERIES*)

A	1	2	3		
B		1	2	3	
C			1	2	3

Letters — singing groups
Numbers — phrases of the round

To avoid the trailing off of the several parts, all voices can end
at a predetermined time or at a signal from the leader. Another device
is to have each of the participating groups sing the round through a
given number of times using the text, and then continue by humming
the melody until given a signal to stop.

(*PREDETERMINED*)

A	1	2	3	1	2	3
B		1	2	3	1	2
C			1	2	3	1

Still another method is to have the entire group join in singing
the final section in unison.

(*CUMULATIVE*)

A	1	2	3	2	3
B		1	2	3	3
C			1	2	3

The placement of singers for each starting group in the round is accomplished by dividing the group by rows (⟌⟍) or files (⁞ ⁞ ⁞ ⁞). When rows are used, it is recommended that the singers in the back row start the rounds so their part can be heard and matched by the other singers. In an informal situation the groups can be divided or segregated by color of hair, of eyes, of shoes, or by month or date of birth. For instance, all those born during the first six months of the year, first; those whose birthday is in the second six months of the year, second.

In the canons that follow, the second voice or group of singers starts a measure later than the first voice, and then follows along in exact repetition of the written melodic line. The starting point for the second voice is indicated in the music by an asterisk.

REUBEN AND RACHEL (CANON)

Reu-ben, Reu-ben, I've been think-ing, What a queer world this would be.

If the men were all trans-port-ed, Far be-yond the North-ern sea.

WHEN JOHNNY COMES MARCHING HOME (CANON)

When John-ny comes march-ing home a-gain, Hur-rah, hur-rah. We'll

give him a heart-y wel-come then, Hur-rah, hur-rah. The

men will cheer the boys will shout, The la-dies, they will all turn out, and we'll

all feel gay when John-ny comes march-ing home.

THE ALPHABET (CANON)

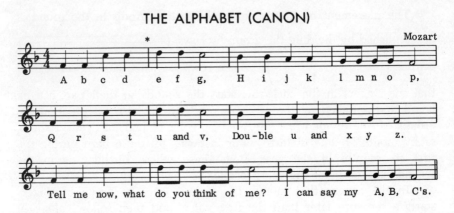

A b c d e f g, H i j k l m n o p,

Q r s t u and v, Dou-ble u and x y z.

Tell me now, what do you think of me? I can say my A, B, C's.

CHANTS OR DESCANTS

A simple chant or recurring pattern of rhythm or melody can give variety and enrichment to a song and at the same time give the singers a feeling for harmonic changes. A chant which changes with the chords of any two chord song can be used by starting on and continuing the first note of the scale as long as possible, then changing to seven of the scale when the first note no longer fits. For instance:

LONG, LONG AGO

Long, long a - go   Long, long a - go   Long, long a - go

Tell me the tales that to

Long, long a - go   Long, long a - go   Long, long a - go

me were so dear   Long long a - go   Long, long a - go

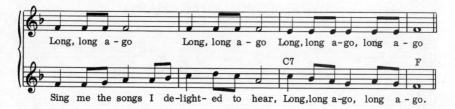

Long, long a - go   Long, long a - go Long, long a-go, long a - go

Sing me the songs I de-light- ed to hear, Long,long a-go, long a - go.

THE MORE WE GET TOGETHER

Traditional

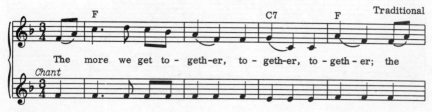

The more we get to - geth-er, to - geth-er, to - geth - er; the

Chant

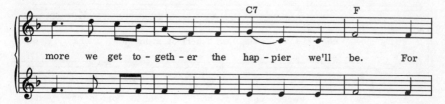

more we get to - geth - er the hap - pier we'll be.   For

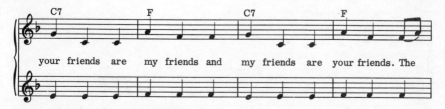

your friends are   my friends and   my friends are your friends. The

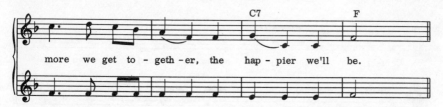

more we get to - geth - er, the hap - pier we'll be.

Sometimes a fragment of melody from the song can be chanted; try "Swing Low, Sweet Chariot" using this chant. Two or four repetitions of the chant make an effective introduction to this song.

SWING LOW, SWEET CHARIOT

Chant
Spiritual

Swing low, cha-ri-ot, swing low, cha-ri-ot, swing low, cha-ri-ot,

Swing low, sweet

swing low, cha-ri-ot, swing low, cha-ri-ot, swing low, cha-ri-ot,

cha-ri-ot, com-in' for to car-ry me home.

swing low, cha-ri-ot, swing low, cha-ri-ot, swing low, cha-ri-ot,

Swing low, sweet cha-ri-ot, com-in' for to car-ry me

Fine
swing low, cha-ri-ot.

home. I looked o-ver Jor-dan and what did I see?

Com-in' for to car-ry me home. A band of an-gels

com-in' af-ter me. Com-in' for to car-ry me home.

44

A similar chant can be developed for "Silent Night" using:

SILENT NIGHT

Descant   Gruber

The three primary chords in the key of C can be used for a chant to accompany Brahms' "Lullaby." The basic form is:

Here is a start on this chant; now continue it with the rest of the song.

LULLABY

A two measure, two part chant for "The First Noel" can be repeated until the refrain or chorus; then everyone sings the regular melody or the harmony parts.

THE FIRST NOEL

Traditional

No - el, No - el; No - el, No - el; No - el, No - el, No -

The first No - el the

el, No - el, No - el, No - el, No - el, No -

an - gel did say was to cer - tain poor shep - herds in fields as they

el, No - el, No - el, No - el, No - el, No - el, No -

lay; in fields where they lay keep - ing their sheep On a cold win - ter's

el, No - el, No - el. No - el, No - el, No -

night that was so deep. No - el, No - el, No -

Unison

el, No - el, Born is the King of Is - ra - el.

el, No - el, Born is the King of Is - ra - el.

47

The descants (chants) included here can be used as an introduction for the songs. Descants can be sung by:

1. A few sopranos while the rest of the sopranos sing the regular melody.
2. A solo voice or solo section while the rest of the choir softly sing or hum the other parts.
3. All the sopranos and tenors while the altos and basses sing the melody in unison.
4. All the women while the men sing the melody in unison.

CHORDAL BACKGROUND

A harmonic background for familiar songs can be provided by three voices sustaining the notes of the chords through humming or singing a neutral syllable. Most rounds can be harmonized by the use of a single chord. In the following round, the first, third, and fifth degrees of the scale supply a suitable chordal background.

ROW, ROW, ROW YOUR BOAT

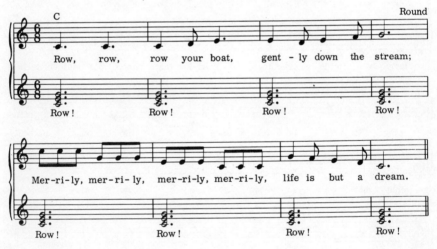

Experienced singers will make chord changes naturally once the first chord has been established, or a chordal accompaniment on piano, uke, or autoharp will assist the singers in hearing changes. In the chapter on song accompaniments, the concept of how to analyze a song for chord changes will be developed.

ACTION SONGS

Another large and practically unlimited area of song enrichment is that of adding actions to songs that are already well known to the singers. The only caution here is that the songs must be thoroughly learned before the actions are added. It may help if the group is divided and some sing while others go through the actions. Visual aids, such as large drawings of objects mentioned in the stanzas, may be helpful in putting across the actions suggested by the songs.

Folk or square dancing to familiar songs sung by the dancers themselves adds much to the enjoyment of a song session. "Looby-Lou" or "Dancing the Hokey-pokey" are illustrations of this type of singing.

SONGS THROUGHOUT THE DAY

There is no limit to the songs that can be used in special situations to build interest and morale. Camps or areas within a camp can adopt or create a song or a stanza for themselves. The routine of the day can be punctuated by songs in all types of informal situations. Here are some examples of songs throughout the day:

WAKE UP SONGS

MORNING IS COME

day is at its dawn - ing The fair - est ev - er seen. The

trum-pets of the morn-ing A - wak - en us from sleep, And

now our good Lord's bless - ing Our joy - ful songs en - treat.

MORNING AND EVENING HYMN

Traditional

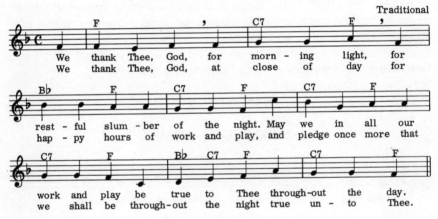

We thank Thee, God, for morn - ing light, for
We thank Thee, God, at close of day for

rest - ful slum - ber of the night. May we in all our
hap - py hours of work and play, and pledge once more that

work and play be true to Thee through-out the day.
we shall be through-out the night true un - to Thee.

MORNING PRAISE

Beethoven

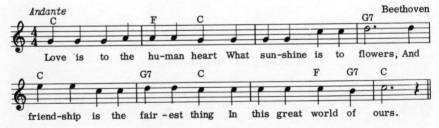

Andante

Love is to the hu-man heart What sun-shine is to flowers, And

friend-ship is the fair - est thing In this great world of ours.

50

BATTLE HYMN OF THE REPUBLIC

Howe

Mine eyes have seen the glo-ry of the com-ing of the Lord; He is tramp-ling out the vin-tage where the grapes of wrath are stored; He hath loosed the fate-ful light-ning of His ter-ri-ble swift sword, His truth is march-ing on. Glo-ry, glo-ry Hal-le-lu-jah. Glo-ry, glo-ry, Hal-le-lu-jah! Glo-ry, glo-ry, Hal-le-lu-jah, His truth is march-ing on.

COME, YE THANKFUL PEOPLE

Elvey

Come, ye thank-ful peo-ple, come, Raise the song of har-vest home; All is safe-ly gath-ered in, Ere the win-ter storms be-gin; God, our Mak-er, doth pro-vide For our wants to be sup-plied; Come to God's own tem-ple, come, Raise the song of har-vest home.

EVERY TIME I FEEL THE SPIRIT

Spiritual

Ev'-ry time I feel the Spir - it mov - in'
in my heart, I will pray; Ev'-ry time I feel the
Spir - it mov - in' in my heart, I will pray.

FOR THE BEAUTY OF THE EARTH

Kocher

For the beau - ty of the earth For the beau - ty of the skies,
For the love which from our birth O- ver and a -round us lies.
Lord of all, to Thee we raise This our hymn of grate-ful praise.

JACOB'S LADDER

Spiritual

We are climb-ing Ja - cob's lad - der, We are
climb - ing Ja - cob's lad - der, We are climb-ing
Ja - cob's lad - der, Sol - diers of the cross.

MY FAITH LOOKS UP TO THEE

Mason

My faith looks up to Thee, Thou Lamb of Cal - va - ry,

Sav - ior di - vine; Now hear me while I pray, Take all my

guilt a -way, O let me from this day Be whol-ly Thine.

O COME, O COME, EMMANUEL

Unison

Traditional

O come, O come, Em - man - - u - el, and ran-som cap-tive

Is - - ra - el; That mourns in lone-ly ex - ile here, un -

til the Son of God ap - pear. Re - joice! Re - joice! E -

man - - u - el Shall come to Thee, O Is - - ra - el.

ONWARD, CHRISTIAN SOLDIERS

Tempo di Marcia

Sullivan

On-ward Chris-tian sol - diers, March-ing as to war,

With the cross of Je - sus Go - ing on be - fore!

Christ the roy-al Mas-ter, Leads a-gainst the foe;

For-ward in-to bat-tle See His ban-ners go.

On-ward, Chris-tian sol-diers, March-ing as to war,

With the cross of Je-sus go-ing on be-fore.

ALLELUIA

Mozart

Al-le-lu-ia, al-le-lu-ia, al-le-lu-ia, al-le-lu-ia.

Al-le-lu-ia, al-le-lu-ia, al-le-lu-ia, al-le-lu-ia.

Al-le-lu-ia, al-le-lu-ia.

KUM BA YAH

Spiritual

Kum ba yah, my Lord, kum ba yah! Kum ba yah, my Lord, kum ba yah! Kum ba

yah, my Lord, kum ba yah! Oh, Lord, kum ba yah!

2. Someone's crying, Lord.
3. Someone's praying, Lord.
4. Someone's singing, Lord.

54

PRAISE TO THE LORD

Traditional

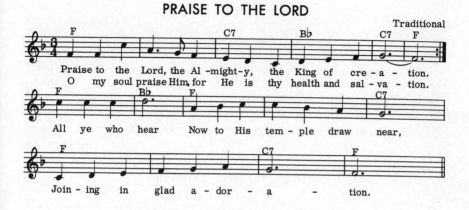

Praise to the Lord, the Al-might-y, the King of cre-a-tion.
O my soul praise Him, for He is thy health and sal-va-tion.

All ye who hear Now to His tem-ple draw near,

Join-ing in glad a-dor-a - tion.

GRACES

PRAISE FOR BREAD

Morn - ing
Noon - time has come, the ta-ble is spread. Thanks be to Him who
Eve - ning

gives us bread; Praise God for bread!

THE FATHER'S WILL

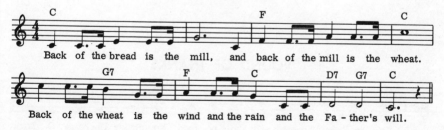

Back of the bread is the mill, and back of the mill is the wheat.

Back of the wheat is the wind and the rain and the Fa-ther's will.

GRACE

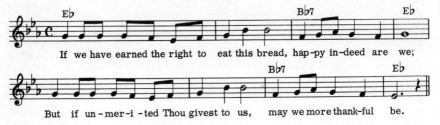

If we have earned the right to eat this bread, hap-py in-deed are we;
But if un-mer-i-ted Thou givest to us, may we more thank-ful be.

HARK TO THE CHIMES

Hark to the chimes, come, bow your head.
We thank Thee, Lord, For this good bread.

GRACE ROUND

We thank Thee for our dai-ly bread, For bless-ings on this ta-ble spread, Our Fa-ther in Heav-en.

ROUND OF THANKS

For health and strength and dai-ly food we praise Thy name, O Lord.

DOXOLOGY

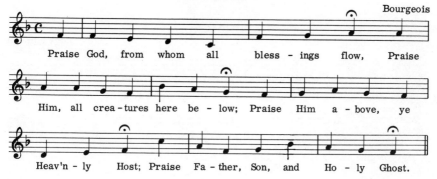

Bourgeois

Praise God, from whom all bless - ings flow, Praise
Him, all crea - tures here be - low; Praise Him a - bove, ye
Heav'n - ly Host; Praise Fa - ther, Son, and Ho - ly Ghost.

HARMONIC GRACE

Fa - ther, we thank Thee now.

THANKSGIVING PRAYER

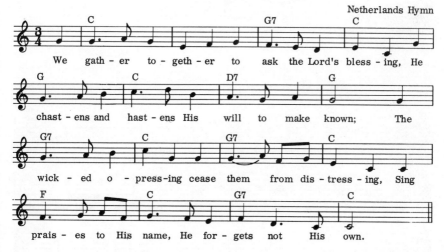

Netherlands Hymn

We gath - er to - geth - er to ask the Lord's bless - ing, He
chast - ens and hast - ens His will to make known; The
wick - ed o - press-ing cease them from dis - tress - ing, Sing
prais - es to His name, He for - gets not His own.

SONGS OF GREETING

HELLO!

Traditional

Hel - lo, hel - lo, hel - lo. We're glad to meet you;

we're glad to greet you. Hel - lo, hel - lo, hel - lo. Hel - lo!

CLAP, CLAP, CLAP YOUR HANDS

Folk Song

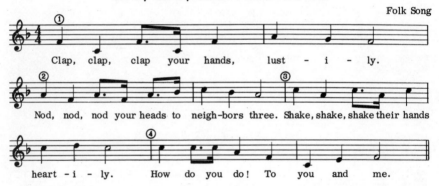

① Clap, clap, clap your hands, lust - i - ly.

② Nod, nod, nod your heads to neigh-bors three. ③ Shake, shake, shake their hands

④ heart - i - ly. How do you do! To you and me.

FOR HE'S A JOLLY GOOD FELLOW

Traditional

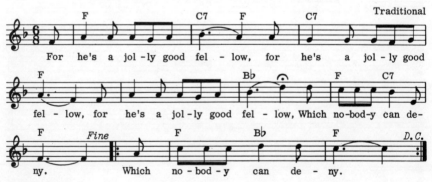

For he's a jol -ly good fel - low, for he's a jol -ly good

fel - low, for he's a jol -ly good fel - low, Which no-bod-y can de-

Fine ny. Which no - bod - y can de - ny.

D.C.

58

HOW DO YOU DO?

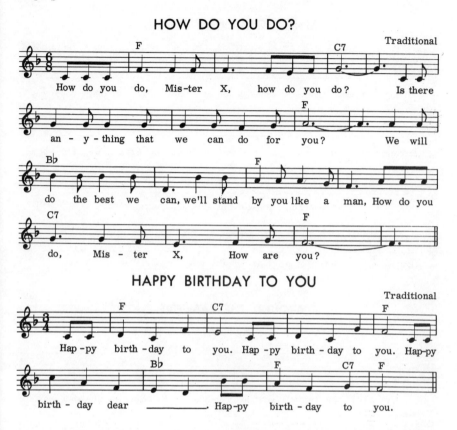

How do you do, Mis-ter X, how do you do? Is there
an - y-thing that we can do for you? We will
do the best we can, we'll stand by you like a man, How do you
do, Mis - ter X, How are you?

HAPPY BIRTHDAY TO YOU

Hap -py birth - day to you. Hap -py birth - day to you. Hap-py
birth - day dear —————. Hap-py birth - day to you.

When this song is used as a general greeting to more than one person, or when the name of the person to whom the song is directed is not known, the words "We bring you this greeting" can be substituted in place of "Happy birthday dear ————." Another device is to sing "Happy birthday, happy birthday, happy birthday to you."

HIKING SONGS

HIKING SONG

I'm nine-ty nine miles from home; I'm nine-ty nine miles from home; I
walked a - while, sat down a - while, I'm nine-ty eight miles from home.

SING YOUR WAY HOME

Traditional

Sing your way home at the close of the day, Sing your way home, drive your trou-bles a - way. Smile ev'-ry mile, for wher-ev - er you roam, it will bright-en your road, it will light - en your load, if you'll sing your way home.

AROUND THE CAMPFIRE

CADIZ

When I was a stu-dent at Ca-diz, I played on my Span-ish gui-tar, Ching, ching. I used to make love to the la -dies, I think of them now from a - far, Ching, ching. Ring, ching, ching, ring, ching, ching, Ring out, ye bells, ring out, ye bells. Ring out ye bells. Ring, ching, ching, ring, ching, ching, Ring out, ye bells, as I played on my Span-ish gui - tar, Ching, ching!

60

COWBOY NIGHT SONG

Folk Song

There's a blue sky way up yon-der; There's a blue sky o - ver my head; There's a blue sky way up yon-der That's a cov-er for my bed; and where - ev - er I wan-der and wher - ev - er I roam, There's a blue sky way up yon-der that's call-in' me home.

DINAH

Traditional

Din- ah, won't you blow? Din- ah, won't you blow? Din-ah, won't you blow your horn? Din - ah, won't you blow? Din - ah, won't you blow? Din - ah, won't you blow your horn? Some-one's in the kitch-en with Di-nah, Some-one's in the kitch-en I know Some-one's in the kitch - en with Din - ah, Play-ing on the old ban - jo. Fe, Fo

fidd - ly I O, Fe, Fo fidd - ly I O, Fe, Fo

fidd - ly I O Play - ing on the old ban - jo.

DO, DO, PITY MY CASE

Folk Song

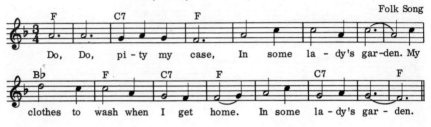

Do, Do, pi - ty my case, In some la - dy's gar - den. My

clothes to wash when I get home. In some la - dy's gar - den.

Clothes to iron
Floor to scrub
Bread to bake

DRINK TO ME ONLY WITH THINE EYES

Folk Song

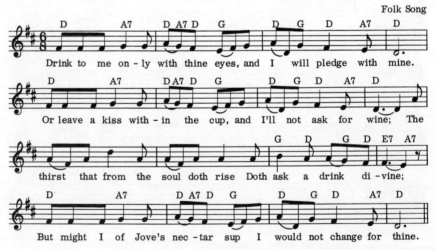

Drink to me on - ly with thine eyes, and I will pledge with mine.

Or leave a kiss with - in the cup, and I'll not ask for wine; The

thirst that from the soul doth rise Doth ask a drink di - vine;

But might I of Jove's nec - tar sup I would not change for thine.

62

EENCY, WEENCY SPIDER

Traditional

Een-cy, ween-cy spi-der went up the wa-ter spout, Down came the rain and washed the spi-der out. Out came the sun and dried up all the rain, And the een-cy ween-cy spi-der went up the spout a-gain.

HOME ON THE RANGE

Folk Song

O give me a home where the buf-fa-lo roam, where the deer and the an-te-lope play, where sel-dom is heard a dis-cour-ag-ing word, and the skies are not cloud-y all day. Home, home on the range, where the deer and the an-te-lope play. Where sel-dom is heard A dis-cour-ag-ing word, and the skies are not cloud-y all day.

OH, DEAR, WHAT CAN THE MATTER BE?

Folk Song

O, dear, what can the mat-ter be? Dear, dear, what can the mat-ter be? O, dear, what can the mat-ter be? John-ny's so long at the fair. *Fine*

He prom-ised he'd buy me a beau-ti-ful fair-ing, a gay bit of lace that the las-sies are wear-ing, He prom-ised he'd bring me a bunch of blue rib-bons to tie up my bon-ny brown hair. And it's *D.C.*

OH, I CAN PLAY

Folk Song

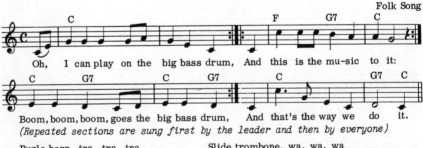

Oh, I can play on the big bass drum, And this is the mu-sic to it:
Boom, boom, boom, goes the big bass drum, And that's the way we do it.
(Repeated sections are sung first by the leader and then by everyone)

Bugle horn, tra, tra, tra
Double bass, zum, zum, zum
Violin, fiddle-dee-dee

Slide trombone, wa, wa, wa
Piccolo, tweet, tweet, tweet
Big bass horn, um-pah-pah

SUMMER EVENING

Folk Song

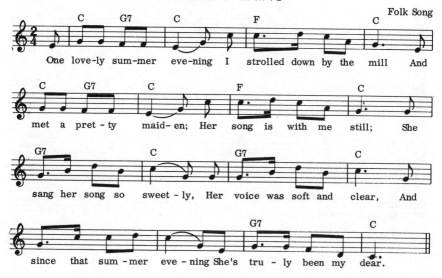

One love-ly sum-mer eve-ning I strolled down by the mill And

met a pret-ty maid-en; Her song is with me still; She

sang her song so sweet-ly, Her voice was soft and clear, And

since that sum-mer eve-ning She's tru-ly been my dear.

SWEET AND LOW

Barnby

Sweet and low, sweet and low, Wind of the west-ern sea; Low, low

Breathe and blow, wind of the west-ern sea; O-ver the roll-ing

wa-ters go, come from the dy-ing moon, and blow, Blow him a-gain to

me, While my lit-tle one, while my pret-ty one sleeps.

O SUSANNA!

Traditional

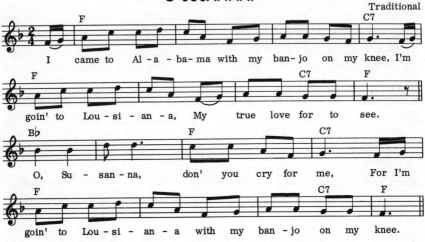

I came to Al - a - ba- ma with my ban- jo on my knee, I'm

goin' to Lou - si - an - a, My true love for to see.

O, Su - san - na, don' you cry for me, For I'm

goin' to Lou - si - an - a with my ban - jo on my knee.

TELL ME WHY

Traditional

Tell me why the stars do shine. Tell me

why the i / - vies twine. Tell me why the

skies are blue, And I will tell you why I love you.

SONGS OF GOODNIGHT AND FAREWELL

ABIDE WITH ME

Monk

A - bide with me! fast fall the e - ven tide, The dark-ness

deep - ens Lord, with me a - bide! When oth - er help - ers fail, and com - forts flee, Help of the help- less, O, a - bide with me.

ALOHA OE

Lilluokalani

Fare-well to Thee, fare - well to Thee, Thou charm-ing one who dwells a-mongst the flow - ers, One fond em - brace be - fore we now de - part, un - til we meet a - gain.

AULD LANG SYNE

Scottish Song

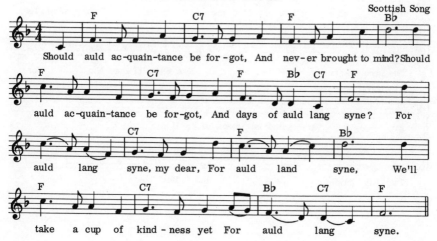

Should auld ac-quain-tance be for-got, And nev-er brought to mind? Should auld ac-quain-tance be for-got, And days of auld lang syne? For auld lang syne, my dear, For auld land syne, We'll take a cup of kind - ness yet For auld lang syne.

CHILDREN'S PRAYER

Humperdinck

When at night I go to sleep, Four-teen an-gels watch do keep,

Two my head are guard-ing, Two my feet are guid - ing, Two are on my

right hand, Two are on my left hand Two who warm-ly

Two are on my right hand Two are on my left hand

cov - er Two who o'er me hov - er Two to whom tis

Two who warm - ly cov - er Two who o'er me hov - er

giv - en To guide my steps to Hea - - ven.

Two who guide my steps to Hea - - ven.

BLEST BE THE TIE THAT BINDS

Nageli

Blest be the tie that binds Our hearts in Christ - ian love; The
fel - low - ship of kin - dred minds is like to that a - bove.

DAY IS DONE

Harrison

Day now is done, there's a star in the west Still is the
land and the twi - light is deep. All things are read - y to
turn to their rest. Fa - ther, Thy love is guard-ing our sleep.

GOOD NIGHT

Round

Good night to you all, and sweet be thy sleep; May
an - gels a - round you their si - lent watch keep. Good-
night, good - night, good - night, good - night.

69

GOOD NIGHT, LADIES

Traditional

Good night, la-dies. Good night, la-dies. Good night, la-dies, we're

going to leave you now. Mer-ri-ly we roll a-long, Roll a-long,

roll a-long, Mer-ri-ly we roll a-long, O'er the dark blue sea.

GOOD NIGHT CANON

Traditional

Glo-ry to Thee, my God this night, for all the bless-ings of the light; keep

me, oh, keep, me, King of Kings, Be-neath Thine own al-might-y wings.

In a canon the second group of singers start one measure later than the first group.

ANGELS WATCHIN' OVER ME

Spiritual

All night, all day, an-gels watch-in' o-ver me, my Lord.

All night, all day an-gels watch-in' o-ver me.

Now I lay me down to sleep an-gels watch-in' o - ver me, my
Lord; Pray the Lord my soul to keep, An-gels watch-in' o-ver me.

MAKE NEW FRIENDS

Round

Make new friends but keep the old;

One is sil - ver and the oth - er gold.

This round may be sung in major or minor mode.

THE STAR-SPANGLED BANNER

O say! can you see, by the dawn's ear - ly light, What so

proud - ly we hail'd at the twi - light's last gleam-ing? Whose broad

stripes and bright stars, thro' the per - il - ous fight, O'er the

ram - parts we watch'd were so gal - lant - ly stream-ing? And the

rock - et's red glare, the bombs burst-ing in air, Gave

proof thro' the   night   that our   flag   was still   there.   O

say does that Star-Span-gled Ban - ner   yet   wave   O'er the

land   of the   free   and the home   of   the   brave.

NOW THE DAY IS OVER

Barnby

Now the day   is   o - ver,   Night is draw - ing   nigh,

Shad - ows of   the ev' - ning,   steal a - cross the   sky.

TAPS

Traditional

Fad- ing light dims the sight   and   a   star gems the sky, gleam-ing

bright. From a - far draw-ing nigh, falls the   night.

FLAG RAISING songs might include "America," "America The Beautiful," "The Battle Hymn of the Republic" and "The Star-Spangled Banner."

WHEN TO SING

Singing can fill the waiting periods of the day. Grace should be sung at mealtime and then a song or two added while individuals are waiting to be served. Another song can be fitted in between the main course and dessert or as an interlude between the meal and the presentation of a speaker or a formal program. When people wait in line, they can pass the time by singing. When a crowd is gathering for an evening program or movie there is another opportunity to start some informal singing, especially if the crowd can be brought into a confined area. A theme song can be used to open or close a regular program or meeting.

These activities can become a tradition in any situation where the same people gather together over a period of time. The problem is to provide the leadership to get the singing started; once it starts, it is very contagious and will practically carry itself with just a suggestion from a leader as to what to sing next.

EQUIPMENT NEEDED FOR SONG SESSIONS

Materials and equipment needed in song sessions will vary with the situation and the objectives to be achieved. A group that has worked together for some time may be able to get along without any visual aids. Mimeographed or printed word sheets are helpful but have the disadvantage of taking the eyes of the singers away from a leader or conductor, thus possibly lessening the precision and spirit that a good leader can elicit. A projector that can operate with a minimum of darkness concentrates attention to one area in which a director can work alongside the screen. Many times a good audio system can be used and the crowd invited to sing along with a record or a tape.

In a more formal situation, it is necessary that song books be in the hands of every one or two singers. The singers should be urged to sit or stand erect and to hold their books high and flat so that everyone can see the music and the leader at the same time. Some leaders use an opaque projector and find it very practical in bringing the attention of all the singers to a central point, in pointing out specific problem areas in a song, and in giving instructions to singers.

A tape recorder with a good microphone is a must for any choir or singing group that aspires to do artistic, expressive work. A single tape made by the group and played back to them is worth hours of talking or countless illustrations by the leader; still the tape recorder must be used with discretion and the group motivated to set their own goals and to improve their work.

When appearing before an audience, members of a choir must give their undivided attention to the choir leader and his direction.

When the attention of all is concentrated on one person, there is little chance for individuals in the group to become nervous or self-conscious. Inattention to the leader is the unpardonable error in any musical ensemble and a mark of a poorly-trained choir.

ACCOMPANIMENT FOR GROUP SINGING

Accompaniments for solo or group singing can have a recreation value of their own over and above their function of pitching the song, setting its mood and tempo, keeping the ensemble together, and accustoming individuals to listen to a part other than their own. There is an aesthetic or enrichment value that comes to the group and accompanist from an artistically played accompaniment, and be it ever so humble, there is no accompaniment more satisfying than one you do yourself!

Clapping is the easiest accompaniment to introduce. There is practically no limit to the variety that can be introduced in this way. Start by reinforcing the primary accent in each measure; then divide the group into smaller sections, with some accenting the first beat of each measure and others clapping on all beats of the measure. Still another segment can try to clap the rhythm of the melody. Some may be able to clap on the off or after beats.

Various sounds can be made by clapping in different parts of the hands or by changing the cupping of the hands. Finger snapping on the offbeat patterns; striking other surfaces or materials with the hands; and repeating sounds on indefinite pitches give variation in the accompanying sounds. For example:

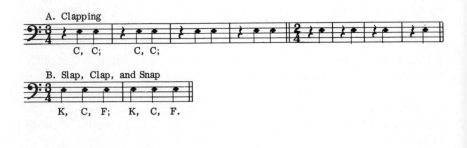

A. Clapping

    C, C;   C, C;

B. Slap, Clap, and Snap

    K, C, F;   K, C, F.

K = Slap the knees.
C = Clap the hands.
F = Snap the fingers.

C. Slap, Snap

K, F; K, F. K, F; K, F.

D. Boom, sh, sh; Boom, sh, sh.

B, SH, SH; B, SH, SH; B, F, F; B, F, F; B, SH; B, SH. B, F; B, F.

B = Say "Boom."
S = Say "sh."

Several people within the larger group can be used to combine or to alternate the suggested rhythmic patterns. Try "Little Annie Rooney" using Examples B and D.

LITTLE ANNIE ROONEY

She's my sweet-heart, I'm her beau,

She's my An-nie, I'm her Joe.

Soon we'll mar-ry, Nev-er to part.

Lit-tle An-nie Roo-ney is my sweet-heart.

These ideas lead quite naturally to the introduction of other percussive articles such as sticks, bottles, nails, spikes, pipes, or gourds as part of the accompaniment for a song. Instruments may become formalized to the extent of being constructed by the players or purchased as a part of the recreational equipment. All of the suggestions given for clapping on various parts of the measure can be applied to percussive instruments. Instruments can be classified as to highness or lowness, lightness, or heaviness, softness or loudness to aid in using them effectively.

Suggestions from the leader and from the group together with opportunities for experimentation usually will stimulate creation of interesting, effective, and entertaining percussive accompaniments for song sessions. Remember, however, that all of these things are not introduced at the same time nor do all of them have to happen at once. Many of them are steps or stages that evolve; they must accompany the singing and not become the chief concern of the performers or the audience.

Melodic instruments used singly or in groups are effective accompaniments for singing. Many times there are capable performers available in a recreational situation; their services surely should be utilized. Instrumentation might range from one of the recorder type instruments (tonette, song-flute, fluto-phone, etc.) harmonica, or bells to any of the instruments used in the regular band and orchestra.

Chordal accompaniments supplied by a group of singers or players are effective. The method of singing a chordal background was presented earlier. This same device could be applied using song or resonator bells struck on the accented beat in each measure. The twelve bar autoharp, which costs approximately $25.00 and weighs about seven pounds, supplies an easy to play and portable means for chordal accompaniments. Chords are produced by simply pressing a button for the chord that is needed with a finger of the left hand and strumming the strings with a pick or with the fingers of the right hand. The only limitations of this little instrument are that it cannot be played in every key and that all chordal combinations are not available on it. It is, however, a useful and usable means of accompanying that should not be overlooked by recreation workers.

Even lower priced and more portable than the autoharp is the ever-popular ukulele. The uke requires more skill on the part of the performer, for he must form each chord with the fingers of his left hand. With a little effort it is possible to learn five or six chords on the uke in a short time, and for those who persist, there is practically no limit to the variety of tunes that can be played. A small four- or six-string guitar has even more volume and more chordal resources than the uke. Either is very useful in a music-recreation occasion.

Accordions have the advantage of portability and versatility. While there are large and small accordions and they differ in their resources, they offer a strong accompaniment or solo possibility for an interested player. Any person who has a good knowledge of the piano keyboard and chords easily can transfer his skill to the accordion. On these instruments one has the advantage of being able to play both melody and chords at the same time, but either the melody or the chords can be used alone to reinforce the voice or other instruments.

Piano is by far the most popular accompanying instrument. Its only disadvantage is that it is not portable. Whenever or wherever a piano is available, it can be a tremendous resource when played by a skilled performer. Ideally the recreational pianist should be competent to play a large variety of songs by ear or from memory, or he should be capable of sight reading the written accompaniments. In situations where only the melodic line is available, the pianist must be able to harmonize the melody with a suitable chordal background. A variety of styles of playing helps to set the proper mood for a song.

The greatest virtue or attribute of a good accompanist is that of following the director and remembering, in most instances, his is an accompanying and not a solo instrument. There are, of course, many times when the accompanist should be given his chance to shine; variety can be achieved by interpolating a solo or a special chorus or two by the accompanist into the song sequence.

When the leader is not playing the accompanying instrument himself, it is recommended that he conduct during the playing of the introduction. This is done to insure the establishment of the correct mood and tempo for the song from the start. The introduction also should establish the pitch on which the singers will start, especially in songs where the melody does not start on the key note or "doh" of the scale.

EVALUATION OF THE SONG SESSIONS

After each song session, the results should be evaluated in terms of what you planned to accomplish. Did you do what you hoped to do? What devices were helpful in drawing the group together? Which songs elicited the best response and were done with the greatest satisfaction by the singers? What changes could be made for a more successful song session? Were instructions understood by the singers? Did the time pass quickly? Through evaluation one can grow in leadership and effectiveness.

Remember, from the leader's point of view, (1) praise will win more converts than criticism, (2) lead, don't follow the group, and (3) enjoy yourself and you usually will gain a response from your singers.

TOPICS FOR DISCUSSION AND ASSIGNMENT

Singing

1. Build a file of songs and resource materials for use in your singing program.
2. Practice playing the melodies for your songs on any instruments that are available.
3. Say the words to songs as you clap the written notation. Play these rhythms on any rhythm instruments that are available to you.
4. Practice placing the pitch high or low with your hands as you sing a song.
5. Examine songs in this book for repetition of the same melodic ideas. Can you distinguish between scale and chordal movement of melodic lines?
6. Sing songs with syllables to develop music reading skill.
7. Make up a chant or descant to be used with a familiar song.
8. Prepare chordal accompaniments on a variety of chordal instruments for songs that you know so that you could play for group singing.
9. Dramatize some of the songs or poems you know. Create dances to be used with familiar songs.
10. Learn the dances that go with songs you sing.
11. Organize a small group to practice singing and conducting recreational songs.
12. Plan song sessions of differing lengths (five, ten, fifteen minutes) for groups of various age levels (elementary, junior high, high school, college, adults) using a variety of themes (patriotic, religious, camping) for formal and informal situations.
13. Conduct the class in a song session. Plan for a definite duration, age group, and recreational setting. Use as many different kinds of materials and approaches as possible.
14. Change minor songs to major and major songs to minor, then try to analyze what the changes do to the mood of the songs.
15. Develop evaluation forms for a long song session from the standpoint of the recreation leader and from the viewpoint of the singer.
16. Plan and create a bulletin board featuring group singing in your recreational program.

RECORDS TO ACCOMPANY AND TO ENCOURAGE SINGING

Another Sing Along	YPR 723
Around the Campfire	YPR 438
Birthday Party Songs	Childcraft 31
Camp Songs	FC 7028
Campfire Songs	Childcraft 20
Children's Sing Along	VL 3680
C'mon You Campers! Let's All Sing	KL 1148
Do — Re — Mi and Other Songs Children Love to Sing	KL 1234
Folk Songs for Camp	FC 7030
Folk Songs for Singing and Dancing	YPR 8005-6
Golden Treasury of Folk Songs	GLP 17
Hillbilly Play Party Songs	Childcraft 19
Hoorah for the Red, White, and Blue	GLP 36
Patriotic Songs and Marches for Children	GLP 1204
Rodgers and Hammerstein Saturday Matinee for Children	GLP 30
Sing Along and Let's All Join In	YPR 15005
The Sing Along Children's Chorus	KL 1177
Songs for Singing	Childcraft 4
Tom Glazer Concert for and with Children	WC 301

Most of this list was suggested by Mrs. George Currlin of the Currlin Music City, 448 S. Winchester Road, San Jose, California.

CHOIR AND CHORUS COLLECTIONS

Fred Waring Song Book	H. Ades	Shawnee Press, Inc., Delaware Water Gap, Penna., 1962
Let's Sing Parts	R. J. Staples	Mills Music Corp., New York, N. Y., 1955

An easy approach to part-singing for beginning choruses. Chords are indicated for all the songs.

Music from Shore to Shore	Leeder & Haynie	Silver Burdett Co., New York, N. Y., 1956
Music the World Sings	Wilson, Leeder, et al	Silver Burdett Co., New York, N .Y., 1952

Two books of program materials arranged for a variety of vocal and instrumental groupings. Suggestions are given for staging and performance.

CHOIR AND CHORUS COLLECTIONS (CONT.)

Rounds and Canons   H. Wilson   Hall & McCreary
                                                Chicago, Ill., 1943

Sixty rounds and canons with good, clear explanatory materials.

Singing Bee   L. Gearhart   Shawnee Press, Inc.
                                                Delaware Water Gap,
                                                Penna., 1956

A collection of 49 songs for two- and three-part treble voices with well-written piano accompaniments. This material will make a strong appeal to singers and audiences alike.

Songfest   H. Simeone   Shawnee Press, Inc.,
                                                Delaware Water Gap,
                                                Penna., 1956

Thirty-four songs for a beginning, mixed chorus. Piano parts are easy to play and the material will gain an enthusiastic response.

Sugar and Spice   H. Ades   Shawnee Press, Inc.,
                                                Delaware Water Gap,
                                                Penna., 1957

Forty, three-part songs for treble voices.

Tunetime for Teentime   I. Cooper   C. Fisher, New York,
                                                N. Y., 1957

This book provides 29 interesting songs for beginning choruses. Part arrangement is flexible, and songs can be used with from one to four parts.

Youth Sings   H. Simeone   Shawnee Press, Inc.,
                                                Delaware Water Gap,
                                                Penna., 1954

Two- and three-part arrangements for mixed voices. Includes patriotic, folk, and sacred songs in good, full arrangements with a solid piano background.

GENERAL SONG COLLECTIONS

TITLE	AUTHOR	PUBLISHER
Get-Together Songs	Lorenz & Eldridge	Lorenz Publishing Co. 209 State St., Chicago 4 Ill., N. D.

GENERAL SONG COLLECTIONS (CONT.)

TITLE	AUTHOR	PUBLISHER
Singing America	Zanzig	C. C. Birchard, Boston, Mass., 1941
Song Session	McLean	Remick Music Corp. New York, 1948
Twice 55 Song Book	Dykema	C. C. Birchard Boston, Mass., (Red Book) 1924 (Brown Book) 1957
Sing Along the Way		Publication Services Nat. Brd., YWCA, 600 Lexington Ave., New York 22, N. Y.
Camp Songs 'n Things		Service Department Box 871 Nashville, Tenn.
The Ditty Bag	Girl Scout Book	Jane E. Tobitt 228 E. 43 St. New York, 17, N. Y.
Sweet Freedom's Song		Cooperative Recreation Service, Delaware, Ohio
Community Sing Session	(101 songs, words only)	Remick Music Corp. New York, N. Y.
Cowboy Songs	(Words and melody)	Remick Music Corp. New York, N. Y.
Freedom Sings	(59 songs, words and melody)	Remick Music Corp. New York, N. Y.

BIBLIOGRAPHY

BOOKS FOR THE SONG LEADER

Will Earhart, "The Eloquent Baton," Witmark, New York, N. Y., 1931.
Helen and Larry Eisenberg, "How to Lead Group Singing," Association Press, New York, N. Y., 1955.
Harry Wilson, "Lead a Song," Hall & McCreary, Chicago, Ill., 1942.

3

Musical Instruments for Recreation

Musical instruments and instrumental instruction can be used in recreational situations for accompanying singers or instrumental performers as a method for developing the recreation leader's own competence on instruments, and as a means of making instrumental instruction available for interested persons of all ages. For these reasons, short sections made up of teaching materials and suggestions for their use on melodic and chordal instruments are presented in this chapter.

An important satisfaction in learning to play any musical instrument is the joy that comes from playing a familiar tune. This enjoyment is a primary objective in recreational music; along with it there should be an increasing understanding of musical symbols and notation so that there is possibility for transfer of skills and for growth in other areas of music.

RECORDER TYPES

Recorder instruments include tonette, song-flute, fluto-phone, ocarina, symphonette, and melody flute. The first four instruments have a range of a ninth (an octave and one pitch) from middle C while the symphonette and melody flute have ranges of two octaves starting from middle C. These instruments can be used by a recreational director to work out the pitches of an unfamiliar song or in introducing a melody to others. Instruction on recorders may start from the third grade upward strictly as a recreational endeavor, for program purposes, or as an introductory and exploratory experience leading to a standard band or orchestra instrument.

To produce a tone on a recorder type instrument, pick up the instrument with the large or bell end away from the body. The seven hole side of the recorder should be up, and the one hole side down. Hold the instrument by forming a letter C with the thumb and first finger of the left hand. Cover the hole closest to the mouthpiece with the pad of the first finger on the left hand and cover the hole on the underside of the instrument with the pad of the left thumb. Be sure to use the pads of the fingers and not the tips, for each tone hole must be completely sealed. Form a reverse C with the thumb and first finger of the right hand, putting the little finger on the last hole of the upper side of the instrument and the right thumb on the underside of the instrument to support it.

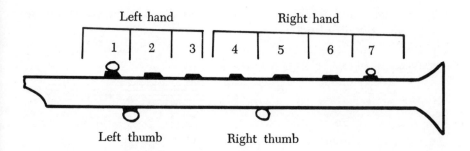

Place the mouthpiece to the lips, take a good, big breath, whisper "toe" and let the breath out slowly while sustaining the "oh" sound. If there are several people playing together, they must listen to each other and match pitches; when a piano is available and it is in tune, use it as a basis for comparison of pitch.

Add one finger at a time from the top downward to establish other pitches. The three fingers of the left hand produce the pitches B, A, and G, and the three fingers of the right hand produce F, E, and D. Remember, spell BAG with the left hand, FED with the right hand, a C at the top, and a C at the bottom. The top C is played with the right thumb alone, while the bottom C is played by adding the little finger of the right hand on the bottom hole to cover all seven holes on the upper side of the instrument. Be sure to cover each hole completely when the fingers are added.

When fingers are lifted, keep them as close to the instrument as possible without altering the pitch or tone quality of the note being sounded. Clap the rhythm of the melody and sing the tune before playing it on the instrument as a means of developing an ability to play the rhythm accurately and to hear the melody exactly in tune.

Fingering for any note can be indicated by using one or two numbers or symbols with this system:

1. Number the fingers from the top downward, one through seven, omitting both thumbs and the little finger of the left hand.
2. The thumb of the left hand is used with every number except O (open) which indicates that no holes are covered.
3. T indicates left hand thumb alone.
4. A single number indicates the number of fingers down.
5. When two numbers are given, first put down the number of fingers indicated by the top number, then add the finger indicated by the lower number. For instance, $\frac{3}{5}$ indicates three fingers and thumb of the left hand down, then add to these just the fifth finger.

The ascending C major scale is fingered:

C	D	E	F	G	A	B	C
7	6	5	4	3	2	1	T

An ascending chromatic scale from D to D is fingered:

D	D♯	E	F	F♯	G	G♯	A	A♯	B	C	C♯	D
6	5	5	4	3	3	2	2	1	1	T	O	O
	7			5		4		4			3	

Practice these familiar tunes on the recorder. Think of the name of the note each time it is played.

MOONLIGHT

TONETTE TUNE

Ⓑ G   D7 G   D7 G D7 G

1 2 3   1 2 3   3 2 1 1 2 2 3   3 2 1   1 2 3   3 3 2 2 1 2 3

LIGHTLY ROW

Ⓒ C   G7   C   G7   C   G7   C   G7   C

3 5 5   4 6 6   7 6 5 4   3 3 3   3 5 5   4 6 6   7 5 3 3   7

TWINKLE, TWINKLE, LITTLE STAR

Ⓓ C   F   C   G7   C   G7   C   G7   C   G7

7 7 3 3   2 2 3   4 4 5 5   6 6 7   3 3 4 4   5 5 6

C   G7   C   G7   C   F   C   G7   C   G7   C

3 3 4 4   5 5 6   7 7 3 3   2 2 3   4 4 5 5   6 6 7

LULLABY

Ⓔ C   G7   C   C   G7   C   *Fine*

5 5 6   7 7   6 6   5 6 7   3 3 4   5 5   6 7 6 5   7

F   C   F   G7 *D.C.*

5 5 4   3 3   2 2   3 4 5   5 5 4   3 3   2 2   3

ABIDE WITH ME

OLD MACDONALD

AMERICA

BEAN PORRIDGE HOT

HOME ON THE RANGE

LONDON BRIDGE

MARY HAD A LITTLE LAMB

PRAYER

EVENING BELLS

REUBEN AND RACHEL

THERE'S MUSIC IN THE AIR (DUET)

WHISPERING HOPE (DUET)

RECORDERS THREE

F.J.B.

All players should practice both the A and the B parts of the duets, and all three parts of the trio, in unison before they attempt to play the numbers with all parts combined. Rhythm instruments or chording instruments can be added to the ensemble as a means of involving more people in the activity.

UKULELE

Ukulele is probably the easiest to play of the fretted, chordal instruments. Hold the instrument against the body with the strings outward, the large part of the uke to the right, and the tuning pegs to the left. Tune the strings starting from the top string downward with the pitches G, C, E, A. If there is no fixed pitch instrument to check by, hum the tune "My Dog Has Fleas" (G, C, E, A). Another device is to establish the first four pitches of the song "Say It With Music," starting from middle C on the piano. Tune the second string from the top to the pitch for "Say," the third string to the pitch for "It," the fourth string to the pitch for "With," and the first string to the pitch for "Music." Check the strings against each other as illustrated.

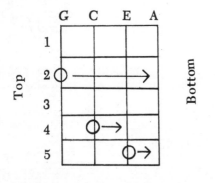

(Frets are the brass strips at right angles to the strings on the finger board of the uke.)

Using a finger of the left hand, press the top or G string of the uke firmly in the space between the first and second fret. Strike the string softly with the ball of the thumb of the right hand, then compare this pitch with that of the open bottom or A string. They should sound exactly the same pitch. Next press the second string from the top, the C string, in the space between the third and fourth fret, and compare its pitch with that of the third or E string. Again, they should sound in unison. Finally press the third string from the top, the E string, in the space between the fourth and fifth fret, and it should sound in unison with the bottom or A string.

With two easy chords it is possible to play an accompaniment for many well-known songs. Number the fingers of the left hand starting with the index finger as one and the little finger as four. Place the neck of the uke between the thumb and first finger of the left hand. Using the tips of the fingers, place the first finger behind the first fret on the third string and the second finger behind the third fret of the first string. This is the F major chord, indicated by the letter F. Next place the first finger behind the first fret of the fourth or bottom string. This is the C seventh chord, indicated by C₇. The diagrams for these two chords look like this:

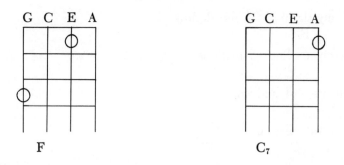

Memorize the hand position for each chord as it is introduced.

Using a felt pick or the ball of the right thumb strum the strings from the top downward, halfway between the neck and the tone hole in the body of the uke, with a firm, quick stroke. Play each chord several times to be sure that the strings sound clearly. Keep both hands relaxed and use the tips of the fingers to form the chords. Next play three F chords in succession followed by three C_7 chords. The pattern is F, F, F, rest, C_7, C_7, C_7, rest, at a moderate, steady speed.

When these changes from one chord to another are mastered, try a song such as "It Ain't Gonna Rain No More" using the F chord until the third "more," then playing the C_7 chord until the last "more." "Long, Long Ago" and "My Maryland" require only these two chords and are very easy to play. Try to hear the chord changes by ear; if this doesn't work, sing the first note of the scale as long as it fits while someone else sings the melody; when one of the scale no longer harmonizes or fits, move down to the seventh degree of the scale and change to the C_7 chord on the uke. This device will work for any two chord melody. Here are a couple of examples; strum the chord indicated on each of the syllables as shown in the diagram.

SKIP TO MY LOU

Choose your partner; skip to my Lou
   F   F

Choose your partner; skip to my Lou
  C_7 C_7

Choose your partner; skip to my Lou
   F   F

Skip to my Lou, my Darling.
  C_7 F F

CLEMENTINE

Oh my darling, Oh my darling
    F   F

Oh my darling Clementine
        F C_7

You are lost and gone forever
        C_7 F

Dreadful sorry, Clementine.
        C_7 F

Check the list at the end of this chapter for other songs that can be played with these two chords in the key of F.

The next step is to learn two additional chords so that these songs can be played and sung in the key of C major. The chord diagrams are:

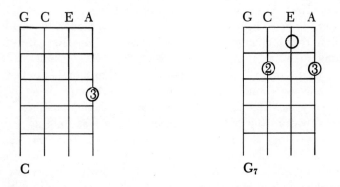

These chords, along with the F major chord, comprise the three primary or principal chords in the key of C. With these chords at your command another long list of songs can be played. Try "Home On The Range" and "Aloha Oe." Hum three, four, and two of the scale as indicated for help on chord changes while someone else plays or sings the melody.

HOME ON THE RANGE

Oh, give me a home where the buffalo roam
    C   C   F   F
    3   3   4   4

Where the deer and the antelope play
```
        C              C      G₇ G₇
        3              3      2  2
```

Where seldom is heard a discouraging word
```
      C         C         F         F
      3         3         4         4
```

And skies are not cloudy all day.
```
      C         G₇        C
      3         2         3
```

ALOHA OE

Farewell to thee, farewell to thee,
```
    F                 C
    4                 3
```

Thou charming one who dwells amongst the flowers;
```
      G₇                           C
      2                            3
```

One fond embrace before we now depart
```
      F         C
      4         3
```

Until we meet again.
```
    G₇          C
    2           3
```

Two chords related to F major are the A₇ and the D₇ chords.

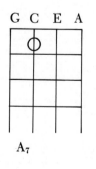

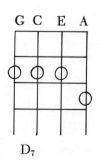

"Dream of Love" can be played using this chordal sequence:

4F, $4A_7$, $4D_7$, $4G_7$, $4C_7$, 2F, $2C_7$;

4F, $4A_7$ $4D_7$, $4G_7$, $4C_7$, 4F.

"Five Foot Two" uses:

4F, $4A_7$, $8D_7$, $4G_7$, $4C_7$, 4F, $4C_7$,

4F, $4A_7$, $8D_7$, $4G_7$, $4C_7$, 2F, $2C_7$, 4F,

$8A_7$, $8D_7$, $8G_7$, $8C_7$,

4F, $4A_7$, $8D_7$, $4G_7$, $4C_7$, 2F, $2C_7$, 3F.

Earlier in this section it was suggested that a pick or the ball of the right thumb be used for strumming the uke. Some variations in strumming can be utilized to make playing more interesting. Use the nail of the index finger for a *down* stroke; then bring the finger *up* across the strings using the ball of the finger. Now use the thumb and the index finger going *down* and just the ball of the finger coming back. Practice this until it can be done smoothly. Try these rhythms or strums in four-four meter:

Beats	1	2	3	4
Strokes	D	D	D	D

	1 &	2	3	4
	D u	D	D	D

	1	2 &	3	4
	D	D u	D	D

These rhythms can be played using all down strokes.

Here are some possibilities in three-four or waltz meters. Try them with "Daisy" or "Sidewalks of New York."

Beats	1	2	3
Strokes	D	D	D

	1 &	2	3
	D u	D	D

	1	2 &	3 &
	D	D u	D u

Again, these can be played with all down strokes.

Thus far the keys of F and C major have been introduced. It is possible to tune the strings of the uke to A, D, F♯, and B; the chord diagrams given for the F and C₇ chords would then sound a whole step higher, becoming the G and D₇ chords.

Another easy way to use these same chord positions in new keys is to employ a device called the capo. The capo fits on any fret of the uke in such a way as to shorten all four strings equally. The player then fingers his chords as before but in front of the capo, and the chords sound in a new key because the strings and the fingerboard have been shortened. Any music dealer who sells ukes should be able to supply a capo.

AUTOHARP

Because it is so easy to play, so portable, and so reasonable in cost, the autoharp can be useful in recreational programs where a chordal accompaniment is needed. In situations where volume is necessary, a microphone and a speaker system can be used to amplify the sound of the autoharp.

Autoharps are shaped like old-fashioned zithers. Chord bars are built in position above the strings of the instrument so that when a chord bar is depressed it dampens or stops the strings not needed in the chord and the others are allowed to sound. Five bar and twelve bar autoharps are manufactured; the twelve bar is strongly recommended for recreational playing.

The 12 chords on the autoharp include the three principal chords used in the keys of C, F, and G major and the keys of d and a minor. When music in other keys has to be adapted to autoharp, move up or down to the closest possible key or to the key that suits the vocal or instrumental range of the other performers.

Place the autoharp on a table with the long side of the instrument toward the body. The fingers of the left hand depress one bar at a time to produce the chord that is needed. Hold a felt pick between the thumb and first finger of the right hand and use it to stroke the strings in a direction away from the body, from the low, large strings to the high, smaller strings. Be sure to press the bar firmly as the strings are stroked with a relaxed, rhythmic hand motion.

The number of times each chord is played and the way it is played depends upon the type of song being used, the effect desired, and the ability of the player. One has a choice of playing only when chord changes occur in the music, on the first beat of each measure, on primary and secondary accents within a measure, or on each beat of the measure.

All of the songs suggested for uke can be played on the autoharp. Collections of songs and books written especially for autoharp will be listed at the end of this chapter.

BELLS

Bells can be used for melodic, accompanying, or chordal patterns with or without other instruments or voices. Manufacturers call their bell sets by various names such as song, resonator, melody, etc. It is recommended that at least a twenty bar, chromatic set be purchased for recreational playing. Each bar or pitch is mounted on a separate block so it can be taken from the case and played individually, thus allowing more than one person to be involved in playing the melody or chords needed.

To accompany a song which uses only the C chord (practically any round) distribute the bells marked C, E, and G. Players grasp the stick of the mallet or beater about a third of the distance from its head for best control, strike the three pitches simultaneously on the first beat of each measure.

The pitches G, B, D, and F form a chord based upon the fifth degree or pitch of the C scale. This chord is indicated as the G_7 or V_7 chord. The C chord and the G_7 chord can be used to harmonize any of the two chord melodies that are suggested in other sections of this book. Again, as with the uke, it is helpful to have the players hum the first degree of the scale so long as it will fit the melody. When this pitch no longer fits with the melody and there is a need to move to the seventh degree of the scale, this is an indication that the chord must be changed.

Next add the pitches F, A, and C to form a chord built upon the fourth degree in the scale of C major. This is the F or IV chord in the key of C and makes available the three primary chords in this key. Using these three chords, C, F, and G_7, one person, or a group of persons, can play an accompaniment for "Home on the Range" by striking the full chord needed at the start of each measure.

HOME ON THE RANGE

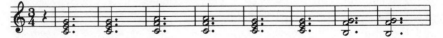

Variation can be accomplished if the player or players strike a note of the chord on each succeeding beat of the measure. (C, E, G; C, E, G; C, F, A; C, F, A; C, E, G; C, E, G; B, F, G; B, F, G; etc.)

HOME ON THE RANGE

Again, try to hear the chord changes by ear.

Counter melodies or descants can be used with Brahms' "Lullaby" and with "Silent Night" to add variety and a different tone color.

LULLABY
Brahms

SILENT NIGHT
Gruber

PIANO

Piano offers unlimited possibilities for years of study by any serious student, but there is no reason why a beginner cannot use limited piano knowledge and skill for his own enjoyment or as an aid in recreational situations. It is possible to accompany any two or three chord songs at the piano by using just the right hand. To do this:

1. Establish the position of C on the piano as the first white key to the left of any series of two black keys. Middle C is usually the first C to the left of the name plate on the piano, or if the piano has a lock, middle C will be the first C to the left of the lock.
2. Place the thumb of the right hand on middle C and then put a finger on each of the four white keys that follow.
3. Number the fingers with the thumb as one and the little finger as five.
4. Press the keys under fingers 1, 3, and 5 all at the same time. This is the C chord; practice it until it can be played with good control.
5. Move the thumb to the next white key on the left; this is the pitch B. Keep the other four fingers in their regular places and play the B along with the keys under the fourth and fifth fingers (F and G). The notation and fingering for these two chords are given here.

Practice this chord change until it can be played smoothly; then try the chordal accompaniment for "John Brown Had a Little Indian."

JOHN BROWN HAD A LITTLE INDIAN

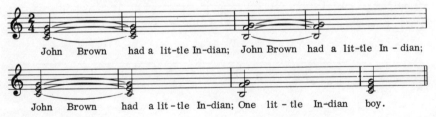

When this can be played with good control and correct rhythm, add a bass note to each chord. The bass note used is the one for which the chord is named. Fingering for the left hand starts with the thumb as 1 and ends with the little finger as 5. The written music is notated as follows:

JOHN BROWN HAD A LITTLE INDIAN

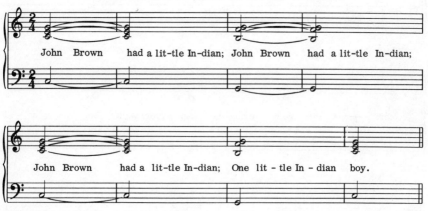

For the refrain or chorus, repeat the entire section once more.

Use "The More We Get Together" as another example; it can be played using the right hand alone.

THE MORE WE GET TOGETHER

Or it can be used with the bass note added.

THE MORE WE GET TOGETHER

A rhythmic variation of these chords can be played by using the bass note on the first beat of the measure and the treble chords on the second and third beats of the measure.

THE MORE WE GET TOGETHER

In order to play the three chord songs listed at the end of this chapter, a chord built upon the fourth degree of the scale is added to the chords already used. In the key of C major, the three chords include these letter names.

$$I = C, \ E, \ G$$
$$IV = F, \ A, \ C$$
$$V_7 = G, \ B, \ D, \ F$$

These chords are notated on the treble staff in this manner:

To avoid the long leaps in going from one chord to the next, it is customary to move each pitch to the nearest chord tone in each chord change. These three chords would be arranged and fingered for the piano in the following manner:

One pitch, the D, is omitted in the piano arrangement of the V₇ chord.

The situation and the facility or skill of the pianist dictate the type of accompaniment that will be played. Again, start with just the right hand chords.

A SPANISH CAVALIER

Hendrickson

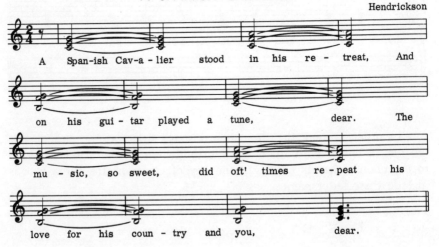

Next the bass note is added, and finally the chord notes are played one after another in an eighth note figuration.

A SPANISH CAVALIER

Hendrickson

A Span-ish Cav-a-lier stood in his re-treat, And on his gui-tar played a tune, dear. The mu-sic so sweet, did oft' times re-peat his love for his coun-try and you, dear.

A SPANISH CAVALIER

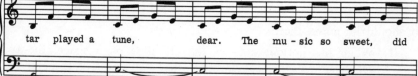

A Span-ish Cav-a-lier stood in his re-treat, and on his gui-tar played a tune, dear. The mu-sic so sweet, did

oft' times re-peat his   love for his coun- try and you,   dear.

Change of key is accomplished by maintaining the same fingering patterns used in the key of C but starting from a different position on the keyboard. In the key of F major the I, IV, and V₇ chords are:

In the key of G major, the three primary chords include:

Notice that once the fundamental position of the I chord has been established, fingerings for these chords are the same in all three keys.

Using the primary chords in these three keys as models, it is possible to build the I, IV, and V₇ chords upon the scale of any major key. For instance, the three primary chords in the key of D major are:

It should be noted that:

1. When the bottom note of the chord is on a space, the two spaces above are used for the other two notes of the chord.
2. When the bottom note of the chord is on a line, the two lines above are used for the other two notes of the chord.

3. When a seventh chord is indicated, as in the instance of the V_7 chord, another line or space is added at the top to the three lines or spaces already used.

Remember if the chord starts on a line, it continues on lines; if the chord starts on a space, it continues to use the space letter names.

When these three chords in the key of D major are used at the piano, the IV chord and the V_7 chord are arranged as before in relation to the I chord of the key, and this results in the hand positions that were introduced in the other keys.

So far chords have been used to accompany a melody which has been sung or has been played on another instrument, but the concept of a fundamental, right hand position can be applied to the playing of melodies, too. Using the pitch G for the thumb position and establishing the key of G major, play the following melody starting with the pitch B under the third finger of the right hand.

The same melody notated in bass clef will sound an octave lower than the treble clef notation and is to be played by the left hand.

Now use the two hands together to play the melody in octaves.

Again, transposition or change of key is accomplished by using the same fingering patterns but starting from a different pitch on the keyboard, just as it was used in chord construction. For the key of

F major the melody would start on the pitch A under the third finger of the right hand.

Next, the left hand chords can be added to the right hand melody.

LONDON BRIDGE

Once chord construction is understood, a shorthand system of notation can be used for piano parts in which only the melodic line and the letter symbols for bass notes and chords are given. A letter name at the beginning of a measure indicates the bass note to be played by the left hand on the first beat of the measure, and also the letter name of the chord to be played by the left hand when and where the symbol "ch" appears above the melody line in the music. Brahms' "Lullaby" requires only three chords, but these are arranged in a new position so they will not interfere with the right hand melody. The chords are notated in bass clef and are to be played by the left hand.

LULLABY

Brahms

Written out completely, the shorthand version would look like this:

Here is "Aloha Oe" in the key of F major; try to work it out using the chords and symbols that are given.

ALOHA OE

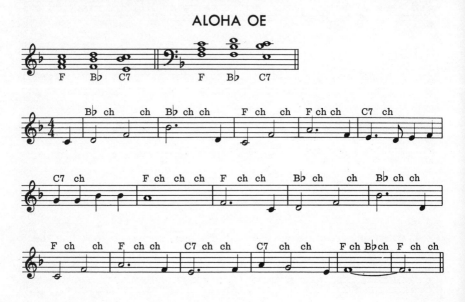

ACCORDION

Accordion, like piano, can be a lifetime study for any serious student who wants to master it, but it isn't necessary to be a virtuoso player to use and to enjoy the accordion. Because of its portability and its flexibility, the accordion is exceptionally well-suited to recreational purposes. Practically all of the devices suggested for the right hand alone on piano can be adapted to use on accordion.

Accordions come in various sizes. The least expensive, standard model is the twelve bass accordion. It generally has a 25-keyed piano keyboard for the right hand and a 12-button keyboard for the left hand. The six buttons closest to the bellows are played with the third finger of the left hand and produce the single pitches of Bb, F, C, G, D, and A from the bottom upward. Middle C, the third button from the bottom, is usually well marked and easily distinguished from the others. The six buttons on the outside, nearest the player, are played with the second finger of the left hand and produce the major chords of Bb, F, C, G, D, and A to coincide with the bass notes played with the third finger. Notice that the three primary chords in each of the available keys are adjacent to each other and can be used to accompany many tunes without adding the melodic line with the right hand.

On the larger accordions with six rows of keys for the left hand, row two is for fundamental basses, row three has major chords, row four has minor chords, row five has dominant seventh chords, and row six has diminished seventh chords. Anyone who is interested enough to buy a good and expensive accordion owes it to himself to secure the best possible instruction from a professional teacher; however, there is no reason why the ideas suggested here for simple, chordal accompaniments should not be used by beginning students.

CHORD CHANGES

Chords and chord changes have been indicated in all of the music presented so far in this chapter. When these guides are not given and one doesn't choose to rely too heavily on his ear, there are some general rules that may be helpful.

1. When 1, 3, or 5 (doh, mi, or sol) of the scale is on the first or accented beat of the measure, use the I chord which is made up of 1, 3 and 5 of the scale (I or tonic chord).
2. When 7 or 2 (ti or re) of the scale is on the first or accented part of the measure, use the V_7 chord which is made up of 5, 7, 2, and 4 of the scale (V_7 or dominant seventh chord).
3. When 6 or 4 (lah or fah) of the scale is on the first or accented part of the measure, use the IV chord which is made up of 4, 6, and 1 of the scale (IV or subdominant chord).

Bear in mind the fact that these are general rules; they won't work every time, because some of the scale pitches appear in more than one chord. If there are other chord pitches in the measure, they can give an addditional indication of which chord to use. In the final analysis, the chord that sounds right is generally the correct chord. This chordal system can be used to simplify a difficult piano part. Remember that every note in the melodic line does not have to be harmonized individually, nor does the harmony always change in each measure.

The number of times each chord is played and the way it is played depend upon the type of song, the effect desired, and the ability of the performer. One may decide to play only when chord changes occur,

or one may play on the first beat of each measure.

Primary and secondary accents within the measure can be stressed through the use of chords.

Occasionally chords will change at irregular times within the measure.

AULD LANG SYNE

Scottish Melody

Rhythmic variation may be used for its own sake. In "Auld Lang Syne" these might be used:

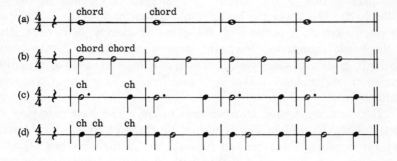

ENSEMBLES

It is possible to have a lot of fun and to give pleasure to others by combining recorder type instruments, jugs, and bottles into a small band. Persons of all ages seem to enjoy playing in or listening to a group of this kind. A start can be made with a band composed of one recorder player, three bottle players, and a jug player.

The jugs and bottles are tuned to these pitches:

Bass G   — one gallon jug, approximately three and one-quarter inches of water

Bass C   — one half gallon jug, approximately three and one-half inches of water

Tenor G   — twelve ounce (7 Up) bottle, empty

Alto B   — "coke" bottle, approximately three-quarters of an inch of water

Alto C   — "coke" bottle, approximately one and one-half inches of water

Soprano E — "coke" bottle, approximately three inches of water

Soprano F — "coke" bottle, approximately three and one-fourth inches of water

Adding water raises the pitch; less water lowers the pitch.

Produce a tone by placing the top of the bottle against the lower lip and whispering "thoe." Direct the air at the edge of the top on the opposite side of the bottle. The larger the opening at the top of the bottle, the lower the bottle is placed on the lower lip. Compare the pitch from each bottle with the piano or melody instrument pitch. If the bottle sounds too low, add more water. If the bottle sounds too high, pour out some water. Do this a little at a time, as a little change in water level makes a big difference in pitch of the small bottles.

Here are some easy arrangements to try. The bass jugs play the bottom line, the middle line is played by three or five bottle blowers, and any number of players can be used on the melodic line. Rhythm instruments can be used together with these jug band arrangements as a means of allowing more people of varying levels of ability to participate.

ROW, ROW, ROW YOUR BOAT

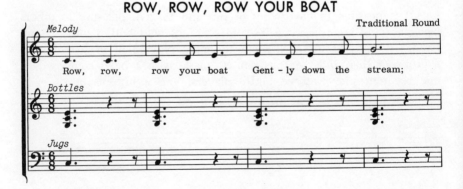

Mer-ri - ly, mer-ri - ly, mer-ri - ly, mer-ri - ly, Life is but a dream.

LIGHTLY ROW

Melody

Bottles

C   G7   C

Jugs

G7   C   G7   C

SWEET MUSIC

Those interested in going beyond this primary stage should refer to Adam Lesinsky's two books on jug bands listed at the end of this chapter.

Ensembles using rhythm instruments can be developed in many situations, and suggestions are given in the chapter on rhythms. Novelty or "Haywire" ensembles, composed of practically any combination of instruments that happens to be available, can be used for campfire or informal programs.

OTHER USES FOR INSTRUMENTS

Experienced recreational workers will recognize the possibilities for using any capable instrumentalist who is available. Trumpeters or performers on other brass instruments should be utilized as buglers to give signals for routine events during the day. A bugle call to awaken campers, to call them to flag-raising ceremonies or to worship, or to play Taps at the close of the day are typical of the functions these players might perform. Capable players can be used individually or in groups for formal or informal presentations; for interludes in song sessions; to provide rhythmic, melodic, or chordal enrichment or accompaniment for poems or songs. They can provide appropriate introductions for songs; introduce new songs; add a harmony part, counter melody, or descant; or add a pitched or unpitched percussive background. Those having the requisite skills can join together for their own pleasure and for the enjoyment of those around them.

Therapists, under proper medical supervision, will find opportunities to provide musical instruments for patients who need to develop muscle strength, endurance, and dexterity.

Above all, don't limit the field in which these materials can be used. They are of interest to many persons of various age groups, and the work of the specialist is to indicate the possibilities and to point out avenues of approach.

FAMILIAR TUNES

These familiar tunes can be harmonized by the use of two or three chords as indicated. The choice of key will be conditioned by the vocal range and the particular instrument used. When in doubt, try the key of F major!

I and V₇ Chords

Ain't Gonna Rain No More
Alouette
Animal Fair
Around the Mulberry Bush
As I was Walking Down the Street
Blow the Man Down
Bridge of Avignon
Clementine
Down in the Valley
Eency, Weency Spider
Go Tell Aunt Rhody
Hot Cross Buns
In and Out the Window
Jim Along Josie
John Brown Had a Little Indian
La Cucaracha
Lightly Row
Little Ducky Duddle
London Bridge

Long, Long Ago
Lovely Evening
Mary Had a Little Lamb
O Christmas Tree
O Du Lieber Augustin
O Where, O Where Has My Little
    Dog Gone
Old MacDonald
Orchestra Song
Polly Wolly Doodle
Rain, Rain, Go Away
Skip to My Lou
Sweet Music
Swing Low
The More We Get Together
There'll Be a Hot Time
This Old Man
What Are Little Boys Made Of?

I, IV and V₇ Chords

Aloha Oe
America
Auld Lang Syne
Away in a Manger
Billy Boy
Blow the Man Down
Brahms' Lullaby
Caissons Go Rolling Along
Camptown Races
Come, Thou Almighty King
Cowboy Jack
Dixie
Down in the Valley
Flow Gently Sweet Afton
For He's a Jolly Good Fellow
Good Night Ladies
Hickory Dickory Dock
Home on the Range
Home Sweet Home
Humpty Dumpty
Jimmy Crack Corn
Jingle Bells
Joy to the World

Juanita
Little Moses
Loch Lomond
Mary, Mary Quite Contrary
Old Lang Syne
O Them Golden Slippers
Pease Porridge Hot
Polly Put the Kettle On
Red River Valley
Reuben and Rachel
Santa Lucia
Silent Night
Soldier, Soldier
Someone's in the Kitchen with
    Dinah
Spanish Cavalier
Sun of My Soul
Taps
There was a Crooked Man
Twinkle, Twinkle Little Star
Vive L'amour
We Three Kings
Whispering Hope

TOPICS FOR DISCUSSION AND ASSIGNMENT

Instruments

1. Play melodies on the piano, song bells, recorder, or any other instrument you play, first using the music and then by ear.
2. Transpose melodies into several different keys and play them on your instruments.
3. Practice playing chordal accompaniments for familiar songs on any instruments that are available to you. Transpose songs into several keys.
4. Develop facility in playing the primary chords in several major and minor keys on piano, uke, or guitar.
5. Harmonize familiar melodies (see page 115-116) using the I, IV, and V chords.
6. Organize a "haywire" orchestra, a "jug-band," or a "folk combo" among your friends and associates.

7. Plan and create a bulletin board to encourage the use of musical instruments for recreation.
8. Refer to the bibliography at the end of this chapter for further reading materials.

BIBLIOGRAPHY FOR MUSICAL INSTRUMENTS

Recorder Types

Margaret Bradford and Elizabeth Parker
How to Play the Recorder
G. Schirmer, Inc., New York, N. Y., 1939
Books I and II for Soprano
Books I and II for Alto
Forrest Buchtel
Melody Fun
Lyons Band Instrument Co., Chicago, Illinois, 1938
An elementary tonette method with words and chord symbols for most of the familiar tunes that are included
Henry W. Davis
Tonette Tunes and Technique
Rubank, Chicago, Illinois, 1941
Dorothy Dushkin
A Method of Study for the Alto Recorder, Book I
Hargail Recorder Music Publisher, New York, N. Y., 1943
Allen Richardson
ONE and ALL
Witmark & Sons, New York, N. Y., 1960
Merrill B. Van Pelt and J. Leon Ruddick
Flutophone Classroom Method
Trophy Products Co., Cleveland, Ohio, 1948
A classroom method with helpful pictures, some piano parts, and some ensemble materials. Progresses rapidly
Fred Weber
Pre-Instrumental Method
Belwin, Inc., Rockville Center, New York, N. Y., 1950
A recorder method which includes autoharp chords

Piano

Michael Aaron
Adult Piano Course, Book I
Mills Inc., New York, N. Y., 1947

Ella Mason Ahearn, et al
 The Adult Explorer at the Piano
  Willis, Cincinnati, Ohio, 1937

J. S. Bach (ed. E. Harold Davies)
 Eighteen Short Works for the Young Pianist
  Oxford University Press, New York, N. Y., N. D.

Dorothy Bishop
 Chords in Action
  Carl Fischer, New York, N. Y., 1956

Charles Cooke
 Playing the Piano for Pleasure
  Harper & Bros., New York, N. Y., 1937

Robert Pace
 Meet the Piano
  Theodore Presser Co., Bryn Mawr, Penna., 1955

Robert Pace
 Piano for Classroom Music
  Prentice-Hall, Inc., Englewood Cliffs, N. J., 1956
   Simplified arrangements of
    America
    Star Spangled Banner
    America, the Beautiful
    Battle Hymn of the Republic

Ernest Schelling, et al
 Beginner's Book for Older Beginners
  Oxford University Press, New York, N. Y., 1929

Robert Shephard
 Harmonizing
  Summy Publishing Co., New York, N. Y., 1956

Hartley D. Snyder
 Music Time
  Fearon Publishers, San Francisco, Calif., 1958
   Easy piano arrangements for musical activities in the pri-
   mary grades. Fifty-one songs classified as holiday, spe-
   cial day, and daily activities.

John Thompson
 Supplementary Piano Course (Melody All the Way)
  Willis Music Co., Cincinnati, Ohio, 1949
   Books 1 a, b; 2 a, b

J. Raymond Tobin
How to Improvise Piano Accompaniments
Oxford University Press, New York, N. Y., 1957

Autoharp

Lillian Mohr Fox
Autoharp Accompaniments to Old Favorite Songs
C. C. Birchard & Co., Boston, Mass., 1947
Beatrice Krone
Melody Fun with the Autoharp
Kjos, Chicago, Ill., 1952

Ensembles and General Collections

Junior Treasury of 100 Well Known Songs
Song Dex, Inc., Box 49, New York 19, N. Y., 1957
Melodic line, words, and chord symbols are given for each song, and only six chords are used in the entire book.
Adam Lesinsky
Fife-jug and Bottle Band
Belwin, Inc., Rockville Center, New York, 1952
Clever arrangements of 20 familiar tunes for jug band. Demands skilled musicians for successful performance.
Ruth Rowen and Bill Simon
Jolly Come Sing and Play
Carl Fischer, New York, N. Y., 1956
Fifteen American folk songs with suggested easy rhythmic and melodic accompaniments.
Lloyd H. Slind
The Play and Sing Book
C. C. Birchard & Co., Boston, Mass., 1956
Materials and suggestions for using instruments along with singing. The 32 selections are taken from "Our Land of Song," Book V in A Singing World School Series.
Paul Sterrett and Scott Wilkinson
You Can Play
Carl Fischer, Inc., New York, N. Y., 1957
Tunes for tonette, ukulele, autoharp, and voices. Twenty-four arrangements are included.
Robert W. Winslow and Leon Dallin
Music Skills
Wm. C. Brown Company Publishers, Dubuque, Iowa, 1958
A general book of music skills

CHAPTER 4

Rhythms

Rhythmic activities provide another large area of recreational participation and can be used as a part of, or as an extension to, singing and instrumental activities. Rhythm is simply defined as a "reoccurring primary accent," but in a musical setting the patterns of primary accents are further complicated by groups of long or short notes superimposed upon and between them. Responses to rhythmic patterns are best expressed in bodily movements, and opportunities for such responses are generally classified as: (1) "free" or "spontaneous" rhythmic movements such as walking, running, skipping, hopping, sliding, and combinations of these; (2) "interpretive" or "dramatic" rhythmic movements which are not prescribed but are suggested by poems, stories, or music; or (3) "prescribed" or "formalized" rhythmic movement such as those found in a dance pattern or in a written score for a rhythm band.

Rhythmic activities will be most useful and will make their greatest appeal to young children, although there are many therapeutic and remedial situations where rhythms could be used for persons of all ages under competent medical supervision and sponsorship.

When we listen to music, we usually respond by tapping our feet, nodding our heads, or in some way keeping time. This steady, reoccurring pulsation is called the *beat*. Even in free rhythms participants must learn to hear, feel, and respond to the beat of the music.

Starting with a simple two or three beat pattern on a drum, tomtom, or a recording, have individuals listen closely with their eyes closed. Then suggest they imitate the beat by clapping softly along with it. Some may wish to stand and mark time with their feet on each drum tap; others may swing their arms in rhythm. Next, have participants walk or march to the music. This should not be in lines or circles but with each individual setting his own pattern in a relaxed, free-swinging gait. Questions should be asked and suggestions made that lead to discovery of "ways" to walk. For instance:

1. Walk as high or low as possible.
2. Walk on the toes or with the toes turned in.
3. Walk with knees bent or with the knees straight.
4. Walk like an old man.
5. Walk like a giant.
6. Walk like boys pulling a wagon.
7. Walk like someone sneaking up on a bird.

The walking activity leads naturally to running and galloping, especially if tempo is quickened. Suggest that participants:

1. Run like a deer.
2. Run so no one can hear.
3. Run like a merry-go-round.
4. Run smoothly, like a top.
5. Run with the knees high.
6. Gallop like a pony.
7. Gallop like a tired old horse.

Together with the activities of walking, running, and galloping are possibilities for hops, jumps, leaps, slides, skips, and combinations of these. Small children may need suggestions or have to be told and shown how to hop by pushing off the floor with one foot and landing on the same foot; to jump by pushing off with both feet at the same time, landing on both feet; to leap by taking long, running steps and by making the steps longer and higher. Ideas such as hopping like a toad or like a rabbit; jumping as though trying to get across a stream or over a fence; skipping slowly, skipping sideways, skipping and turning, skipping backwards, skipping while crossing one leg over the other, skipping high and then low, skipping like a bouncing ball; sliding smoothly as on ice — all help to get individuals started and to give variety to free rhythms.

Some members of the group will listen for and recognize heavy or accented beats in the rhythmic arrangement and will mark them with a heavy step, by bending the knees as the marked steps are taken, by swinging one or both arms, or by clapping their hands in rhythm. Awareness of the basic beat can be developed through the use of poetry. Try to give every word of "Hi Diddle Diddle" the same amount of stress; it quickly degenerates into a monotonous, uninteresting sound. Now say the rhyme naturally, and notice how some words are given more stress than others and that these stressed words fall into regular groups or patterns.

In music composition these beats or patterns are marked off into units of twos or threes and are called measures. They indicate the reappearance of a heavy or primary accent known as the rhythm of the measure. Variation in the rhythmic patterns is the first step in eliciting changes in bodily response. The change could be as simple as a change in direction, or it could involve a complete change of movement patterns. Change in the size of a response can be indicated by a circular motion in the air or by drawings such as these:

2 meter

3 meter

4 meter

Another phase in developing rhythmic awareness can be accomplished through imitation. Ask individuals to say their names and then to clap the rhythm of their names or play them on a percussive instrument. Send a rhythmic message to be transmitted from person to person in the group; after the rhythmic figure has been picked up or "received" by someone of the group, the person who "received" the message can transmit a new or changed message to the next person in the group.

Rope jumping and rope turning develop a feeling for rhythm and could be used in many recreational situations to prescribe activities that children enjoy. Rope turners and spectators chant the rhymes and the actions to be executed by the jumper. Some rope skipping rhymes are:

A.   Teddy bear, teddy bear, turn around;
      Teddy bear, teddy bear, touch the ground;
      Teddy bear, teddy bear, tie your shoe;
      Teddy bear, teddy bear, now skiddoo!

      Teddy bear, teddy bear, point to the sky;
      Teddy bear, teddy bear, wink your eye;
      Teddy bear, teddy bear, pull your wig;
      Teddy bear, teddy bear, dance a jig.

A-1. (Variation. Can be used with all the lines above)
      Teddy, teddy, teddy,
      Turn around, 'round, 'round;
      Teddy, teddy, teddy,
      Touch the ground, ground, ground.

      Teddy, teddy, teddy,
      Show your shoe, shoe, shoe;
      Teddy, teddy, teddy,
      That's enough for you.

B.   Old lady, old lady, touch the ground;
      Old lady, old lady, turn around;
      Old lady, old lady, point your shoe;
      Old lady, old lady, 23 skidoo!

C. Johnny, Johnny went to France
    To teach the ladies how to dance;
    First the heel and then the toe,
    Spin around and away you go!

D. Spanish dancer, do the split;
    Spanish dancer, give a high, high kick;
    Spanish dancer, turn around;
    Spanish dancer, get out of town.

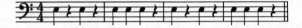

Use this well-known drum beat or cadence to introduce pre-scribed rhythms and response to orders or commands. Orders should be given and executed in rhythm; the tempo or speed of the cadence may vary to fit the circumstance. Stay on a given pattern until it is well established by the group, then try another.

Participants march in rhythm with the cadence then respond to a suggestion to clap, to hop, or to jump in time with the drum beat. Combinations such as these supply variation:

1. March, march, turn a-round.
2. March, march, clap your hands.
3. March, march, tap your shoulders.
4. Clap, clap, stamp your feet.
5. Jump, jump, swing your arms.
6. Hop, hop, march, march, march.

The beat of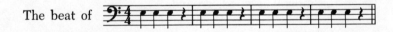

could be interpreted:

1. Clap, clap, hop.
2. Hop, hop, turn.
3. Swing, your arms.
4. March, march, stop.

Some groups could do a series of these one after the other, taking directions from printed signs or from a blackboard.

Interpretive or dramatic rhythms are closely related to free rhythms. They call for expressive movements and activities which are not prescribed but are suggested by the mood of a sound pattern, a musical composition, or any experience the group would like to interpret and share. This could involve assuming a role, acting out a poem or story, interpreting a story or a musical composition, or devising an appropriate accompaniment of bodily movements to heighten the expressiveness of a poem or story.

Just the suggestion of playing the role of a traffic policeman; a bicycle rider; a skater; a swimmer; a boatman rowing; a baker mixing a cake; a painter painting a fence; a cowboy swinging a lariat; a cobbler hammering, sewing, or shining shoes; an elephant in a parade; or a lion in the forest could start a chain reaction of rhythmic activities in an assemblage of children. Interpreting or imitating the sounds of small and large clocks helps to develop a concept of fast and slow speeds. Introduction of different-sized bells can lead to perception of high and low or fast and slow sounds. Here are some familiar rhymes suitable for dramatization in rhythmic play:

1. Here we go up, up, up,
   Here we go down, down, down,
   Here we go backward and forward,
   And here we go around, 'round, 'round.

2. Polly, put the kettle on, Polly, put the kettle on,
   Polly, put the kettle on, We'll all have tea.
   Polly, take it off again, Polly, take it off again,
   Polly, take it off again, They've all gone away.

3. Rock-a-by, baby, on the tree top,
   When the wind blows, the cradle will rock,
   When the tree bends, the cradle will fall,
   And down will come baby, cradle, and all.

4. There were two blackbirds sat on a hill,
   One named Jack, and the other named Jill.
   Fly away, Jack, fly away, Jill;
   Come back, Jack, come back, Jill.

5. Leg over leg, the dog went to Dover;
   When he came to a stile, jump! he went over.

6. Once I saw a little bird
   Come hop, hop, hop;
   I cried to the little bird,
   "Stop, stop, stop,"
   I was going to the window
   To say, "Howdy-do,"
   But he shook his little head,
   And away he flew.

7. Look at my dog. I call him Pink.
   Now sit up, Pink, and do not wink,
   Look in my eyes! Steady, steady!
   Hear the command! Are you ready?
   Now, sir, attend!   When I say four,
   You'll walk three steps, and shut the door!

Experiences that induce enough enthusiasm will call for repetition and practice to clarify the ideas expressed; however, it is important that this be done within the limits of the children's interest and attention spans.

ACTION SONGS

These well-known songs and the directions given with them are illustrative of resources that can be developed using familiar materials. Chord changes are indicated, and the keys were chosen because of their suitability for uke, autoharp, or piano.

ROW, ROW, ROW YOUR BOAT

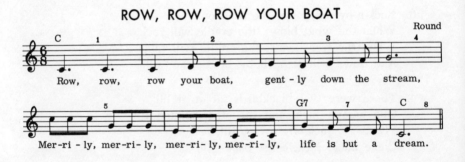

Directions:

    Sit in chairs or on the floor.

    Pretend to hold a pair of oars in your hands.

    Sway forward and back in rhythm with the music

    as though rowing a boat.

CANOE SONG

Our pad - dles keen and bright Flash- ing like sil - ver
Dip dip and swing them back Flash- ing like sil - ver

Fol - low the wild goose flight Dip dip and swing.
Swift as the wild goose flies Dip dip and swing.

Directions:

    Sit in chairs or kneel on the floor.

    Pretend to hold a paddle in your hands.

    Swing the paddle in rhythm on the first

    and third beats of each measure.

    Paddle first on one side, then on the other.

This song can be sung as a round or as a canon in either the major or minor mode. Sing the first measure loud, the second measure soft, the third measure loud, and the fourth measure soft.

TEN LITTLE INDIANS

One lit-tle, two lit-tle, three lit-tle In - dians, four lit-tle, five lit-tle,

six lit -tle In -dians, seven lit -tle, eight lit-tle, nine lit-tle In -dians

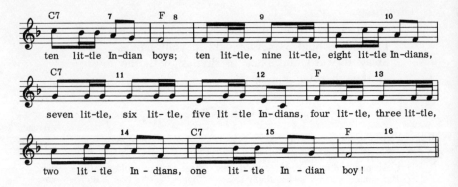

ten lit-tle In-dian boys; ten lit-tle, nine lit-tle, eight lit-tle In-dians,

seven lit-tle, six lit-tle, five lit-tle In-dians, four lit-tle, three lit-tle,

two lit-tle In-dians, one lit-tle In-dian boy!

Directions:

Players count off in tens.

Each group of ten form a single line or file.

Each person may have a chair behind him.

Players sing the song, and as each number is said,

the person having that number sit or squats in his place.

As the number is said the second time, the person having that number stands.

Change places and numbers and try it again at a faster speed.

MULBERRY BUSH

Here we go round the mul - ber - ry bush, the

mul-ber-ry bush, the mul-ber-ry bush; here we go round the

mul - ber-ry bush, so ear - ly in the morn - ing.

Directions:

Join hands and form a circle.

Measures 1-6 Skip to your right.

Measures 7-8 Turn around where you are.

On the other stanzas, go through the motions of doing the task described, then turn around on the last two measures.

This is the way I brush my teeth
This is the way I wash my face
This is the way I comb my hair

BYE BABY BUNTING

Bye ba-by bunt - ing, dad - dy's gone a - hunt - ing to
get a lit -tle rab -bit skin to wrap the ba-by bunt- ing in.
Bye ba - by bunt - ing; bye ba - by bunt - ing.

Directions:

Measures 1- 4   Sway to and fro as though rocking a baby.
Measures 5- 8   Place your left foot forward and aim your gun.
Measures 9-12   Run forward and pick up rabbit you have shot.
Measures 13-16 Wrap the baby in the rabbit skin.
Measures 17-24 Sway to and fro.

RIDE A COCK HORSE

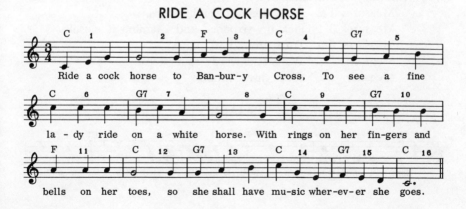

Ride a cock horse to Ban-bur-y Cross, To see a fine
la - dy ride on a white horse. With rings on her fin-gers and
bells on her toes, so she shall have mu-sic wher-ev- er she goes.

Directions:

Form a circle or a single line standing side by side.

Measures 1- 8 Gallop forward eight times.

Measures 9-10 Raise your hands above your head and shake your fingers.

Measures 11-12 Bend forward and touch your toes.

Measures 13-14 Turn around in your place.

Measures 15-16 Bow from the waist.

CROOKED MAN

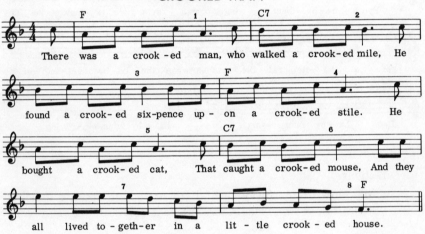

There was a crook-ed man, who walked a crook-ed mile, He
found a crook-ed six-pence up - on a crook-ed stile. He
bought a crook-ed cat, That caught a crook-ed mouse, And they
all lived to - geth-er in a lit - tle crook - ed house.

Directions:

Walk like an old, crooked man. Use a cane and an old hat if they are available.

Measures 1-2 Walk forward eight steps.

Measures 3-4 Pick up sixpence and examine it closely.

Measures 5-6 Turn around in place.

Measure 7   Walk backwards four steps.

Measure 8   Clap three times.

SNAIL

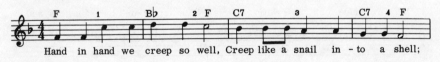

Hand in hand we creep so well, Creep like a snail in - to a shell;

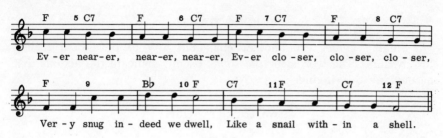

Ev - er near-er, near-er, near-er, Ev-er clo-ser, clo-ser, clo-ser,

Ver - y snug in - deed we dwell, Like a snail with - in a shell.

Directions:

Join hands in a single line. Follow the leader into a circle.
The leader forms a spiral bringing the players closer together
until they are "wound up." The players reverse and march
back to their original positions.

HUMPTY DUMPTY

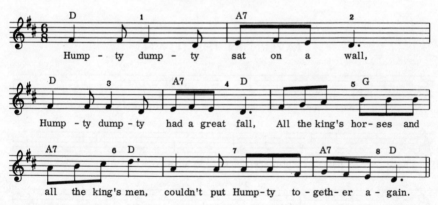

Hump - ty dump - ty sat on a wall,

Hump - ty dump - ty had a great fall, All the king's hor - ses and

all the king's men, couldn't put Hump-ty to - geth- er a - gain.

Directions:

Form a single line standing side by side.
Measures 1-3   Sway from side to side seven times.
Measure 4   Squat on the word "fall."
Measures 5-6   Gallop forward as though riding a horse.
Measures 7-8   Back into original places, hands folded, looking
               sad, and shaking your head.

SINGING GAMES

Singing games are another enjoyable way to develop a feeling for rhythm. The words for the songs usually indicate the actions that accompany the singing.

MULBERRY BUSH

My head, my shoul - ders, my knees, my toes; My head, my shoul-ders, my knees, my toes; My head, my shoul-ders, my knees, my toes, my shoul - ders, knees, and toes.

TAVERN IN THE TOWN

My head, my shoul-ders, knees, and toes. (KNEES AND TOES) My head, my shoul-ders, knees, and toes. (KNEES AND TOES) Heads and shoul - ders, knees and toes; my head, my shoul - ders, knees, and toes. (KNEES AND TOES)

BINGO

Directions:

1. Sing the song as written.
2. Sing the song to BINGO: clap on the B and sing (spell) I N G O. Sing the last Bingo.
3. Same as two, but clap on B and I and sing N G O.
4. Clap on B I N and sing G O.
5. Clap on B I N G and sing O.
6. Repeat the song as before up to B I N G O. Clap out B I N G O, and sing the last Bingo.

Other names and other stanzas may be substituted in place of BINGO. For instance:

"There is a driver on our bus, and Billy is his name-o."

Or the rhythm might be changed to:

"There is a leader in our camp, and Thelma is her name-o."

The rhythm in the second section of the song would be

T H E, L M A.

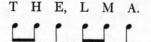

FOLK DANCE

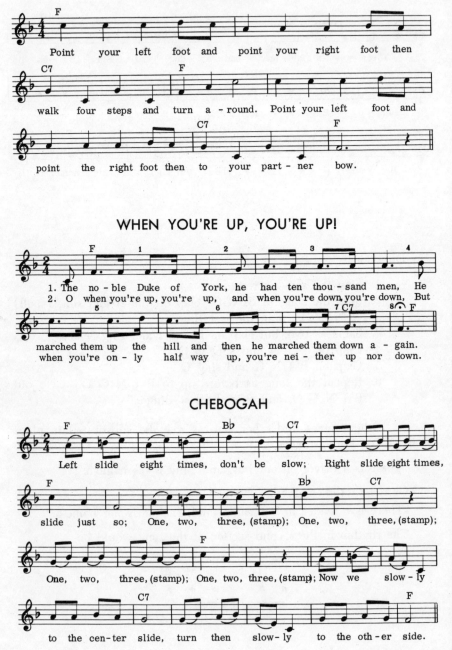

Point your left foot and point your right foot then
walk four steps and turn a - round. Point your left foot and
point the right foot then to your part - ner bow.

WHEN YOU'RE UP, YOU'RE UP!

1. The no - ble Duke of York, he had ten thou - sand men, He
2. O when you're up, you're up, and when you're down, you're down, But

marched them up the hill and then he marched them down a - gain.
when you're on - ly half way up, you're nei - ther up nor down.

CHEBOGAH

Left slide eight times, don't be slow; Right slide eight times,
slide just so; One, two, three, (stamp); One, two, three, (stamp);
One, two, three, (stamp); One, two, three, (stamp); Now we slow - ly
to the cen - ter slide, turn then slow - ly to the oth - er side.

SANDY MALONEY

Can you dance, San-dy Ma - lon - ey? Can you dance, San-dy Ma - lon-ey?

Can you dance, San-dy Ma - lon - ey, As we go round and round.

2. Here we go, Sandy Maloney.
3. Put both your hands on your shoulders.
4. Put both your hands behind you, etc.
    A. Join hands and skip in a circle.
    B. Change in direction of skip for each stanza.

Other singing games, with directions, follow.

DANCING SONG

Place your right foot for-ward so To the front we all then go.
Then your left foot for-ward place, and go skip - ping back in place.

Tra- la- la -la la - la tra -la -la, Tra-la-la -la la - la Tra-la la.

Directions:

    Join hands and form a circle.
    Measures 1-4 Follow the directions of the song.
    Measures 5-6 Skip to the right.
    Measures 7-8 Skip to the left.
        NOTICE THAT EACH SECTION IS REPEATED.

DANCE WITH ME

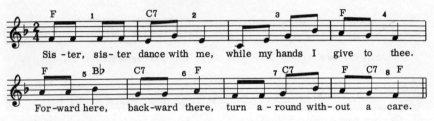

Sis -ter, sis - ter dance with me, while my hands I give to thee.

For -ward here, back -ward there, turn a - round with- out a care.

Directions:

Form double lines with couples facing each other.

Measures 1-2   Bow to your partner.

Measures 3-4   Take your partner's hands.

Measures 5-6   Take a sliding step to the right and to the left.

Measure 7   Drop your hands and turn around.

Measure 8   Stamp your feet three times.

SWINGING

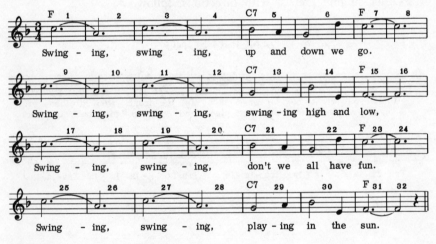

Swing - ing,   swing - ing,   up   and   down we   go.

Swing - ing,   swing - ing,   swing -ing high and   low,

Swing - ing,   swing - ing,   don't we   all   have fun.

Swing - ing,   swing - ing,   play - ing   in   the   sun.

Directions:

Form a single line side by side.

Measures 1- 4   Step forward and swing your arms as though
pushing a swing.

Measures 5- 8   Run forward four steps as though running under the swing.

Measure 9-12   Turn and repeat measures 1-4 from the other side.

Measures 13-16   Run back to your original position.

BEAN PORRIDGE HOT

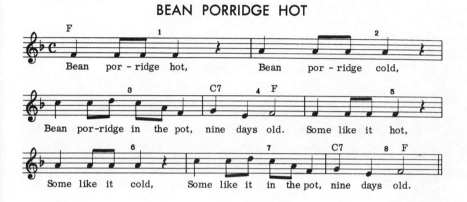

Bean por - ridge hot,   Bean por - ridge cold,

Bean por-ridge in the pot, nine days old.   Some like it hot,

Some like it cold,   Some like it in the pot, nine days old.

Directions:

Form a double line or circle facing partners.

Measure 1   Strike your knees, clap your hands, and touch your partner's hands.

Measure 2   Repeat measure one.

Measure 3   Place your hands on your hips and turn around in place using four steps.

Measures 5-8   Repeat the first four measures.

HUNTING SONG

A - hunt-ing we will go,   a - hunt- ing we   will go,

heigh - ho   the   mer -ry - o,   a - hunt- ing we   will   go.

Directions:

Form two lines facing each other; all of those in line sing and clap their hands in rhythm.

Two people at the top of the line join hands.
They skip to the bottom of the line and back.
They separate and run behind the other players to the bottom of the line, taking places at the bottom of the line.
Repeat with the next couple.

AWAKE YE SLEEPING SHEPHERDS

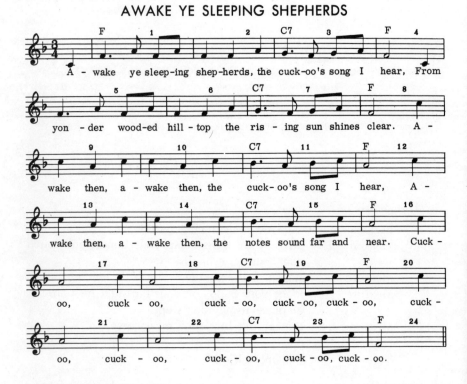

A - wake ye sleep-ing shep-herds, the cuck-oo's song I hear, From yon - der wood-ed hill - top the ris - ing sun shines clear. A - wake then, a - wake then, the cuck- oo's song I hear, A - wake then, a - wake then, the notes sound far and near. Cuck - oo, cuck - oo, cuck - oo, cuck - oo, cuck - oo, cuck - oo, cuck - oo, cuck - oo, cuck - oo, cuck - oo.

Directions:

Count off by twos.
Odd-numbered persons squat or sit on the floor and rest their heads on their hands as though sleeping.
Even-numbered persons join hands, form a circle around the others and sing as they skip to the right.
When the singers reach measure 13 and sing "Awake then, awake then," the sleepers arise, join hands and skip to the left.

At measure 13 those in the outer circle stop and clap their hands in rhythm while they sing.

HICKORY DICKORY DOCK

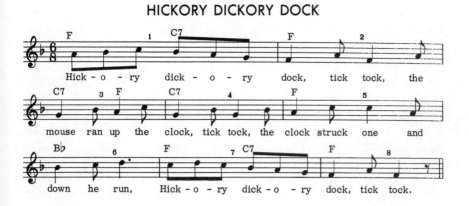

Directions:

Form a circle or a single line standing side by side.

Measure 1   Swing your arms like a pendulum.

Measure 2   Put your hands on your hips and stamp twice.

Measure 3   Run forward three steps.

Measure 4   The same as measure two.

Measure 5   Clap your hands twice.

Measure 6   Run back to your original position.

Measure 7   Swing your arms again.

Measure 8   Put your hands on your hips and stamp twice.

RHYTHMIC INSTRUMENTS

It is assumed that rhythmic instruments are already being used in the recreation program since they were previously suggested as accompaniment and enrichment of singing activities. It was noted that rhythm instruments are an extension of the hands in order to add variety of tone colors, pitch, and dynamic levels to a song session. It was recommended that only a few instruments should be introduced or used at a time, and that their use should be allowed to evolve as steps or stages for the embellishment of the recreational music program.

The use of instruments in the recreation program might have come about through the introduction of sound effects to heighten the impact of a story; they may have been used to reinforce the rhythm of a nursery rhyme or a poem that was well-enough liked to be repeated and elaborated.

Now comes the time to amplify the ideas for the use of rhythm instruments that were previously mentioned as accompaniments to other activities. The recommendations that follow can lead to the use of instruments (1) in a formalized ensemble, (2) with singing, (3) with piano, or (4) with recorded music.

Remember, all of these ideas will not fit into every situation, nor need they all to be used at one time. Take plenty of time to develop rhythmic concepts and be sure to keep the ideas simple for a beginning group. It may take months to accomplish all the skills listed here, but these suggestions should serve as starting points.

1. Play a recording or sing a song ("Susie, Little Susie," Page 142) for the group. Have them listen carefully for a definite beat in the music.

2. Have the listeners respond to the music by clapping their hands, swinging their arms, or marching about the room to the rhythm of the music. Most of the listeners will probably feel the rhythm of the steady, recurring pulse or beat in the music.

3. Develop an awareness of the mood and spirit of the music. Is the music light or heavy, happy or sad, soft or loud, fast or slow, lilting or martial, bright or dark, cheery or gloomy? Have individuals demonstrate these qualities of the music by their actions.

4. Introduce the rhythm instruments by playing them, calling attention to the characteristic tone quality, giving their names, and demonstrating how each instrument is held and played.

5. Decide which instruments would fit best with the music.

   a. Which instruments sound light and which sound heavy?
   b. Which instruments sound high and which sound low?
   c. Which instruments are easiest to play softly and which are easiest to play loudly?

6. Distribute a *few of one kind* of instrument and instruct the members of the group in its use.

   a. Place instruments on the floor or in the lap.
   b. Pick up instruments on a signal from the leader.
      (This may be a verbal, visual, or aural signal. Some leaders use a high pitched tone or chord for a signal to pick

up the instruments and a low pitched tone or chord to put the instruments down.)

   c. Start and finish playing together on a signal from the director.

7. Establish the *rhythm of the beat* (the regular, steady beat that keeps going just like the tick of a clock) using just one type of instrument on every beat. Usually the less resonant instruments such as rhythm sticks, sand blocks, or jingle clogs are used for this purpose. This may be as far as the group will want to go in one session.

8. Establish the *rhythm of the measure* (the accented beat that usually falls into patterns of two, three, or combinations of twos or threes). This is the primary accent or *one* of each measure. At first it may be advisable to have all the players try to clap this beat. Then when a few individuals exhibit the capacity to hear the rhythm of the measure and keep it steady while the others play the rhythm of the beat, a limited number (more could be overpowering) of deep, resonant instruments such as tom-toms, large drums, or temple blocks can be distributed to these individuals for their use on their rhythm of the measure.

9. Establish the *rhythm of the melody* (the pattern of melody suggested by the words in a song or by the melody of an instrumental composition). This rhythm usually is played by high, light instruments such as triangles, bells, tambourines, or jingle clogs.

Be sure to review how the instruments are held and played and when they are to be played. Seldom are all of the instruments used or played at the same time. Some authorities suggest that only those instruments regularly found in a symphonic band or orchestra such as the triangle, tambourine, drums, and cymbals be used; others advocate the use of rhythm instruments such as rhythm sticks, sand blocks, shakers, triangles, and tom-toms that can be made and decorated by the performers.

RHYTHM SCORES

Using only the instruments of the orchestra, try this instrumentation on the following score.

SUSIE, LITTLE SUSIE

Su - sie, lit-tle Su-sie, now here is some news! Geese are run-ning

bare-foot be - cause they've no shoes. The cob-bler has leath-er but

no last to use. So he can-not make them a pair of new shoes.

A. All voices or melody instruments, line one
B. Tambourines on the rhythm of the beat, line three
C. Drum on the rhythm of the measure, line four
D. Triangle on the rhythm of the melody, line two

Experiment with combinations of these, such as A-B, A-C, A-D, then A-B-C-D.

Another instrumentation uses instruments the player could build or decorate.

A. All voices or melody instruments, line one
B. Rhythm sticks on the rhythm of the beat, line three
C. Tom-tom on the rhythm of the measure, line four
D. Shakers on the rhythm of the melody, line two

Try various combinations of these rhythms along with the melodic line.

Subdued or delicate passages sound best accompanied by light, high-pitched instruments on the accented beats of the measure, on the rhythm of the melody, or on fragments of the rhythm taken from the melody. Climaxes in the music are indicated by cymbal crashes, struck tambourines, or heavy drum beats. The instruments must be played softly at all times in order that the performers can hear the music and each other.

Most of this activity has been at the rote or imitative stage. Performers have experimented with instruments singly and in combinations and have participated in decisions as to what combinations of instruments they liked best; then they have depended upon memorization in subsequent performances.

As the group progresses to longer and more complex music, a written score can be developed by placing pictures or symbols over the words where the instruments are to be used.

Rhythm sticks |

Tom-toms   ⊔

Triangles   △

Rests   •

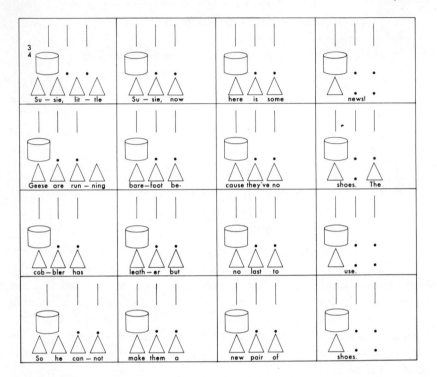

Standard notation and note values can be introduced with a line score for the percussion instruments.

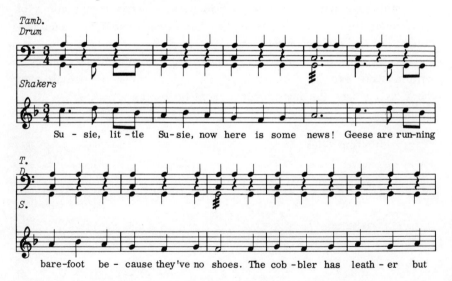

no last to use. So he can-not make them a pair of new shoes.

Words give important clues about repeated sections in the music. Performers should be aware of repetition and should decide whether or not identical sections are to be played the same way on each repetition. This is a start toward an understanding of musical notation and the ability to follow a written score. Scores can be written on a blackboard, on poster paper, or ·they can be mimeographed so each participant has a copy for his own use.

Be sure to give the performers many opportunities to hear the music before they try to develop their own scores. Perhaps they should orchestrate only one strain at a time even though they are familiar with the entire composition or recording. Awareness of repetition, contrast, and variation (the three elements of musical form) is developed by looking for and listening to phrases or sections of the music that are repeated.

CONCEPTS LEARNED THROUGH RHYTHMS

In addition to the musical concepts developed through rhythmic activities, participants should develop awareness of tempo (fast-slow), pitch (high-low), dynamics (loud-soft), mood (gay-sad), and the ability to respond physically to rhythmic patterns. Exposure to rhythmic experiences leads to social skills such as the ability to work and play with others, to take instruction and follow directions, to share and take care of equipment, to an extended attention span, and to the sharing of experiences that have given satisfaction. The individuals learn factual materials, but more important, they learn to enjoy, to imagine, to create, and to know something of their capacity to participate in many new and interesting rhythmic activities.

RHYTHMIC ACTIVITIES FOR ADULTS

Older children and adults can develop a "rhythm band" for a campfire or program stunt, but with younger groups care must be taken to avoid too much use of time on the "rhythm band" phase of recreational program in a bid for repeated public performances for cheap publicity. Those who have a special interest and training in rhythms or with percussive instruments should consider the possibilities of percussion ensembles for recreation. There is available a rich literature of American Indian, Latin American, African, and contemporary music that should be challenging and stimulating for players of all levels of proficiency. This music is graded and listed in the solo and ensemble lists compiled and published by the Music Educators National Conference.

For older persons there are the possibilities of rhythmic activities in close-order drill; folk, square, and social dancing; modern and interpretive dancing; and calesthenics to music.

RHYTHM ACTIVITIES AND RECREATION CRAFTS

Rhythm activities and a recreational crafts program combine into an interesting project. Salvaged and expendable materials are utilized to make satisfying and useful instruments that can be used time after time in the recreational situation or that can be taken home by the participants who build them. The project should be limited or expanded to meet the local situation and the interests, experiences, or backgrounds of the individuals involved.

Examples of the use of salvaged materials follow:

1. Large spikes or bolts of various sizes can be struck together.
2. A small coke bottle can be struck lightly with a large nail. Vary the pitch by putting water in the bottle.
3. A cow bell, with or without its clapper, can be held in the hand and struck with a large nail.
4. Discarded brake drums can be painted with aluminum paint, suspended from a durable peg, and struck wtih a wooden or rawhide mallet.

Other basic and inexpensive instruments can be built using a few simple tools.

1. Rhythm sticks
    a. Cut half-inch, hardwood dowling into one-foot lengths.
    b. Smooth the ends and sides of the sticks with fine sandpaper and wipe clean of dust.
    c. Paint with bright colored enamels.

2. Clavis
   a. Cut one inch, hardwood dowling into six-inch lengths.
   b. Smooth ends and sides of the sticks with sandpaper.
   c. Varnish with a hard-finish varnish.
3. Coconut shells
   a. Saw coconut in half.
   b. Scrape it out and let it dry.
   c. Drill two small holes in the top of the coconut halves for cord handles.
4. Sand blocks
   a. Cut 2x1 lumber into four-inch lengths.
   b. Sand and round the edges of the blocks.
   c. Thumb tack emery paper onto the blocks.
5. Shakers
   a. Box
      (1) Put about 20 beans in a kitchen match or similar box. (3x6x1 /2 inches)
      (2) Scotch tape or cement the ends to keep the box closed.
      (3) Color or decorate in any way desired.
   b. Tin
      (1) Fill a small tin, such as a baking powder can with a fitted lid, about a quarter full of beans or rice.
      (2) Cement the lid to make it solid.
      (3) Color or decorate as desired.
   c. Bells — Attach small sleigh bells to nine- or ten-inch strips or loops of tape or leather and use as wristlets and anklets.
6. Drums
   a. Body
      (1) Choose any hollow container of suitable diameter and depth.
      (2) Sand, round, or smooth the surfaces on which the heads are to be placed to avoid sharp edges which might cut the heads.
      (2) Experiment with single-and double-drums.
   b. Heads
      (1) Select sections of inner tubes, parchment paper, linen, or animal skins. Contact your local music instrument repairman for discarded drumheads.
      (2) Cut paper patterns with enough overlap to properly secure the heads on the drums.

(3) If skin heads are used, soak them in tepid water until they are soft. Wring out as much water as possible, and then fasten the head securely in position on the drum. It will shrink and harden as it drys.

c. Fasten heads to the drum by:
   (1) Tacking
       (a) Stretch the wet drumhead over the end of the drum.
       (b) Look at the top of the drum as though it were the face of a clock.
       (c) Place a tack at the positions of 12, 6, 3, 9 in that order.
       (d) Be sure to pull the drumhead tight and smooth before placing a new tack.
       (e) Place tacks at positions of 1, 7, 4, 10, drawing drumhead tight and smooth for each position.
   (2) Wrapping a strong cord or wire around the drum just below the top edge. Pull the drumhead tight and smooth.
   (3) Using an embroidery hoop to hold the drumhead in place.
   (4) Using a network of string, leather, or shoe lacings to secure the head to a solid band in the center or bottom of the drum.
   (5) Lacing two drumheads together from top to the bottom of the drum.
       (a) Cut paper patterns for the drumheads and punch holes for the lacings.
       (b) Using the pattern cut both drumheads at once and punch holes for the lacings.
       (c) Use temporary lacings to hold the drumheads in position while the permanent lacings are bestrung.

d. Beaters for the drum
   (1) The fingers or hands can be used to tap the drum.
   (2) Medium-hard tympani sticks can be purchased at any music store.
   (3) Beaters can be made by:
       (a) Cementing a small, sponge-rubber ball onto the end of a length of half-inch dowling.

(b)   Wrapping a ball of string or yarn onto the end
of a one-foot length of dowling or a notched
rhythm stick, covering the ball with a piece of
chamois or flannel, and tying it securely in place.

More ideas for building rhythm instruments can be found in the reference materials listed at the close of this chapter.   The book "Invitation to Rhythm" by James Clemens (Wm. C. Brown Co. Publishers,
1962) is especially recommended.

TOPICS FOR DISCUSSION AND ASSIGNMENT
Rhythms

1. Build a file of materials such as scores, pictures, music, and record
lists for use in the rhythms program.
2. Develop evaluation forms for a recreational rhythms program from
the standpoint of the leader and from the standpoint of the listener.
3. Learn the words to some of the folk and square dances you do.
4. Learn and practice calls for square dancing.
5. Develop a rhythm band among your associates; take turns in direct-
ing the group and developing scores for the band to play.
6. Plan and create a bulletin board featuring rhythmic activities for
recreation.
7. Read books and magazine articles about rhythmic activities and
write a short summary of these materials for your own file.

BIBLIOGRAPHY FOR RHYTHMS
Rhythmic Activities

Francis Arnold
    Arnold's Collection of Rhythms
        Willis Music Co., Cincinnati, Ohio, N. D.
Gladys Andrews
    Creative Rhythmic Music for Children
        Prentice-Hall, New York, N. Y., 1954
Lois M. Butler & Barbara A. Reed
    Dance & Play Activities for the Elementary Grades
        Chartwell House, Inc., New York, N. Y., 1951
Julia M. Buttree
    The Rhythm of the Redman
        Ronald Press, New York, N. Y., 1930

Mary Carmel
  Music Rhythms and Games
    Follett Publishing Co., Chicago, Ill., 1952
James Clemens
  Invitation to Rhythm
      Wm. C. Brown Co. Publishers, Dubuque, Ia., 1962
Lottie E. Coit & Ruth Bampton
  Follow the Music
    C. C. Birchard & Co., Boston, Mass., 1948
Satis N. Coleman
  Creative Music in the Home
    L. M. Meyers, Valparaiso, Ind., 1928
Angella Diller & Kate S. Page
  Rote Pieces for Rhythm Band
    G. Schirmer, Inc., New York, N. Y., 1930
Grace Fielder
  The Rhythmic Program for the Elementary School
    Mosby, St. Louis, Mo., 1952
Frank H. Geri
  Illustrated Games & Rhythms for Children
    Prentice-Hall, Inc., New York, N. Y., 1955
Alice Hamlin & Margaret Guessford
  Singing Games for Children
    Willis Music Co., Cincinnati, Ohio, 1941
Margaret N. H'Doubler
  Movement and Its Rhythmic Structure
    Kramer Business Service, Madison, Wisc., 1946
Beatrice H. Hill
  Starting a Recreation Program in a Civilian Hospital
    National Recreation Association, New York, N. Y., 1952
J. C. Jobson
  Toy Orchestra Tunes
    Boston Music Co., Boston. Mass., 1938
Ida Krarvitz and Robert Kerr
  How to Teach Rhythms and Rhythm Bands
    G. Schirmer, New York, N. Y., 1955
Dorothy La Salle
  Rhythms and Dances for Elementary Schools
    Ronald Press, New York, N. Y., 1951

Ardelle Manning
    Original Children's Activity Songs
        A. Manning, Box 1250, Palo Alto, California, 1959
            Recording available
Bernard S. Mason
    Drums, Tomtoms, and Rattles
        A. S. Barnes, New York, N. Y., 1938
Eva Mirchin
    Let's Have a Rhythm Band
        Sam Fox, New York, N. Y., 1958
            Columbia record Cl 1026 has the same title and supplements the book.
M. Renstrom
    Rhythm Fun
        Pioneer Music Press, Salt Lake City, Utah, 1957
Mary S. Shafer
    Rhythms for Children
        Ronald Press, New York, N. Y., 1938
Lloyd H. Slind
    Play and Sing Book
        C. C. Birchard & Co., Boston, Mass., 1956
Rhoda R. Sutton
    Creative Rhythms
        A. S. Barnes & Co., New York, N. Y., 1949
Lillian Vandervere
    Picture Scores
        C. C. Birchard & Co., Boston, Mass., 1928
Lyravine Votau
    Rhythm Band Direction
        Pan-American Band Instrument Co., Elkhart, Ind., 1951
Marcelle Vernazza
    Making and Playing Classroom Instruments
        Fearon Publishers, San Francisco, California, 1959
Augustus D. Zanzig
    Starting and Developing a Rhythm Band
        National Recreation Association, New York, N. Y., 1948

Packets

Games for the Elementary Grades
    Hazel Richardson
        Burgess Publishing Co., 426 S. 6th St., Minneapolis 15, Minn., 1955

A valuable source of playground and recreational materials on 3 1/4 x 5 1/2 inch cards.

Rhythmic Activities, Series 1 & 2
    Frances R. Stuart and John S. Ludlam
        Burgess Publishing Co., Minneapolis 15, Minn., 1955
            Two packets, each containing 50 dances and singing games. Suitable for use with elementary school children. Music and directions on 3 1/4 x 5 1/2 inch cards.

Activity and Rhythmic Recordings

Fun With Rhythm
    Dr. L. G. Mersen and Catherine F. Reilly
        Mercury Sound Books 60008-9-10
            8A Fun With Rhythm — Autumn Leaves
            8B Let's Skate — Cinderella
            9A Happy Thanksgiving — The Christmas Party
            9B My Dolly — Happy Easter
            10A Fiesta — Winter's Frolic
            10B Curtsy and Bow — Our Feathered Friends
                Piano and rhythm instruments with narrated suggestions. Several complete lessons are given. Well chosen and played.

Holiday Rhythms
    #8302 Wood and Tarner
        Bowman Records, L. A.
            Going Home From School   May Day
            Hallowe'en   Valentine Day
            Thanksgiving   Birthday March
            Christmas   Easter
            Washington's and Lincoln's Birthdays

I Am A Circus
    Children's Record Guild 1028
        Children have an opportunity to participate as members of a circus. Kindergarten to third grade.

Indoors When It Rains
    Children's Record Guild 1021
        Use this material for listening and to suggest activities. Kindergarten to third grade.

Lead a Little Orchestra
    Columbia MJV4-115

Let's Have a Rhythm Band
 Columbia Cl 1026
  There is a booklet of music and instruction published for use
  with this recording.
Little Indian Drum
 Young People's Records 619
  Useful in developing a sense of rhythm. Story with narration,
  songs, and sound effects with orchestral accompaniment.
  Children can participate in imitative rhythmic play. Ages
  2 to 5.
The Merry Toy Shop
 Children's Record Guild 1022
  Children imitate toys to rhythmic music. Kindergarten to
  third grade.
Mexican Folk Dances
 Bowmar Records, L. A.
  Six easy dances with complete instructions.
The Musical Mother Goose
 Children's Record Guild 209
  This record can be used for rhythmic activities. Kindergarten
  to third grade.
Nothing to Do
 Children's Record Guild 1012
  Activity record suggesting marching, jumping, tip-toe, skating,
  up and down, clapping, tapping, rocking, and spinning songs.
  Voice with accompanying instruments. Kindergarden to third
  grade.
Out of Doors
 Young People's Records 724
  This is an activity record that can be used in the classroom.
  Kindergarten to third grade.
The Party Record
 Allegro AJ 11
  Kindergarten to second grade.
Play-a-long Songs
 Caravan C 15
  Kindergarten to second grade.
Play Party Games
 Bowmar Records, L. A.
  Two albums contain 21 song dances of the United States.

Rhythmic Activities
    Whitney's, 150 Powell St., San Francisco
        Record 1000 A-B
            Walk, skip, walk with change of direction
            Slide, heavy and light walk, small run, gallop, big run
        Record 1001 A-B
            Swings, turn-walk-hold, bounce and swing, run-jump
            Run and leap, walk to run to fall, bounce-preparation for
            jump, and jump
        Record 1002 A-B
            Polka and Waltz
            Music for rhythmic dramatization
                Original piano music by Florence Bassett with sug-
                gestions and directions for their use by Cora Chest-
                nut.
Rhythm is Fun #8300
    Bowmar Records, 4921 Santa Monica Blvd., L. A. 29, California
        Moore, Schubert, and Dexter
            Record 1
                Basic locomotor rhythms (even and uneven)
                Walk, run, uneven rhythms, accent, changes of speed,
                reviews
            Record 2
                Walk, run, hop-jump or leap, gallop, skip, slide
            Record 3
                Swing high swing low, away we go
                Repetition, mysterious
                    Drum beats. Excellent leaflet of suggestions for
                    use.
The Rhythms of the World FP 740
    Folkway Records and Service Corp., N. Y.
        Narrated by Langston Hughes
Rhythm Time #8301, Wood & Tarner
    Bowmar Records, L. A.
        Basic Rhythms
        Combinations
        Mechanical Rhythms
        Circus
                Piano
Ring Around the Rosey
    Allegro AJ 3

Sidewalk Songs
  Mercury 32
Singing Games and Folk Dances
  Bowmar Records, L. A. #B201 — B206
    B204 — From Around the World
    B205 — American
    B206 — Latin-American
      Total of 69 dances included. The albums are pro-
      gressively difficult. Printed instructions with all al-
      bums. Oral, walk-through instructions for those listed.
Skip to My Lou
  Allegro AJ5
    Kindergarten to third grade.
Square Dances for Children
  Peter Piper
  Columbia 4-147
Strike Up the Band
  Children's Record Guild 5027
    Children have a chance to participate in a rhythm band. Kin-
    dergarten to third grade.
Swing Your Partner
  Young People's Records 9002
    Good introductory recording for folk dancing. Kindergarten
    to sixth grade.
Teddy Bear's Picnic
  Columbia MJB54
Toy Symphony
  Young People's Records 1001
    This is the music of Joseph Haydn and is good for listening
    as well as for rhythms. Third to seventh grades.

CHAPTER 5

Listening

Music appeals in various ways to individuals, depending upon their previous background, experience, and exposure to music and upon the listeners' immediate wishes and needs in the realm of music. The response one makes to music can be physical, emotional, or intellectual (foot, heart, or head), or it may be a combination of these depending upon the listener's needs at a given time. Generally speaking, the richer and more varied a person's musical background, the greater will be his chances for a satisfying and enjoyable response to music and for making an intelligent and adequate choice of musical experiences.

The degree to which musical experiences create a desire in the listener to relive an experience or to seek further experiences in this media, the degree to which the listener becomes sensitive to and discriminating in his responses and choices of musical experiences, to those degrees can it be said that the learner is learning to appreciate music.

When one stops to think about it, all music participation depends upon the participant's ability to hear and to listen accurately and critically. Singing, playing instruments, participating in rhythmic activities all demand an ability to listen. Through listening comes the ability to recognize and respond to the rhythmic, tonal, dynamic, melodic, and harmonic elements of music. The advent of radio, television, and high fidelity recordings has made it a comparatively simple and easy matter for individuals to experience and share music far beyond their own performance ability or that which may be available at concerts in their own communities.

An interested and musically-informed recreation director will be aware of the contribution that well-planned listening activities can make to his program. He will provide enjoyable and stimulating listening experiences to help his clients acquire the information and understanding necessary to guide them in making competent choices and judgments as music consumers. When planning the music listening program, the recreation director will keep in mind:

1. the musical background and experience of his clients
2. the response he expects from the listener. (Is this to be an active or a passive listening experience?)
3. the contribution that music is to make in this situation. (Is music in the foreground or background of the listener's consciousness?)

He will consider possibilities for using music as a soft, pleasant background for other endeavors; as an accompaniment for participation in other recreation activities; or for the sheer pleasure of listening and enjoying live or recorded performances of music.

BACKGROUND MUSIC

Background music may help to while away the hours and contribute to the well-being of listeners in a variety of situations and settings. For example, soft music could be used in hospitals during visiting hours, at dinner time, for afternoon rest periods, or for Sunday religious services. In public rooms or in places where ambulatory patients gather, a centrally controlled system with speakers in each room can be used. In wards or in private rooms, individuals should be able to turn the speakers on or off and to control volume levels. Pillow speakers are available, and with transistor radios, small earphones similar to those on hearing aids are usable. Penal institutions could make effective use of similar facilities.

Camps, national or state parks, playgrounds, and community centers could provide music at mealtimes, during craft activities, for chapel services, and for any period when people congregate or wait. When music is transmitted from a central control area, the persons operating the equipment must work with their consumers to select materials and volume levels. The law of diminishing returns sets in rapidly; music at a constant, high volume level may soon become something to shout over. In some localities good salon music is broadcasted from FM stations for many hours of the day without interruption of commercial announcements; this is an excellent source of low cost background music.

MUSICAL ACCOMPANIMENT

Recorded or live music is an essential element for dancing, synchronized swimming, marching, or drilling, stunts, dramatizations, shows, or plays. Mood music can be used for rest or story telling periods, for social gatherings, and for athletic contests; but care and discrimination in the choice of music and in the quality of sound reproduction are vital factors that can add or detract from the musical effect and the enjoyment of everyone involved.

MUSIC FOR LISTENING

More formalized programs for the sheer enjoyment of listening to live or recorded music may fit into the recreational program in the following ways:

1. Weekly listening sessions for the entire family conducted in conjunction with other recreational activities at neighborhood recreation centers.
2. Regularly-scheduled concerts of recorded music planned to attract varying age and interest groups. These concerts can be heard in recreation centers or in private homes. Problems of suitable audio equipment can be solved by making adequate, portable record players available to the groups. Simple, easy-to-serve refreshments at the close of the sessions make for a social, friendly atmosphere.
3. Groups that meet regularly to listen to or to view outstanding broadcasts. The Metropolitan Opera broadcasts and the Standard School Broadcasts are examples of worthy programs.
4. Study groups that gather to preview music to be featured at concerts in the community. Watch church and school calendars for free programs, especially during the holiday seasons. Private music teachers are always glad to have an audience for their student recitals, and in college communities faculty and student concerts provide highly rewarding opportunities to hear competent soloists and ensembles free of any admission charge.
5. A group to attend artist concerts in the community under professional guidance could be pleasurable and exciting. Pre-registration and prepayment of fees on a seasonal basis are usually necessary to insure against losses because of absences when tickets have to be bought and paid for in advance. These sessions could be presented in cooperation with adult education

and college extension departments or with other recreational, cultural, and educational agencies in the community.

While the primary objectives for most recreation listening are amusement, pleasure, and enjoyment, these outcomes are attained also through social development of the individual in relation to the social group or environment in which he finds himself. Generally, a pleasurable exposure to music will be conducive to greater interest and understanding and there will be a tendency to seek further opportunities for emotional and intellectual responses to music. These experiences in turn become the basis for awareness, growth, value judgments, and a general ability to recognize and appreciate excellence in a variety of types of musical compositions and performances.

In *How to Listen to Good Music*[1], McKinney and Anderson liken this process of musical communication from creator to performer to consumer to that of the transformation of energy. Music "which exists first in the mind of the composer . . . is conveyed by the singer or the pianist, the orchestra or the choir to the listener, who reabsorbs this musical medium into his own experience as his own image, idea, thought, or emotion." The problem as they see it is "that of keeping the efficiency loss at a minimum in transmission." Some recommended procedures and activities for helping the recreation leader achieve a successful transmission of ideas in a listening session are:

1. Give a variety of direct experiences using many types of music. Relate the programs to the interests, skills, and backgrounds of participants. Use questionnaires or interviews for gathering information to formulate a schedule of events or of listening units. It is mandatory that music experiences start where the listeners are, but it is also essential that the participants derive a feeling of growth from their experiences. Use the old, favorite music, but plan to present something new and different at each listening period.

QUESTIONNAIRE FOR MUSIC APPRECIATION

Name _____ Date _____

PERFORMANCE SKILLS

Indicate if you now (N) or formerly (F) participated in any of these music activities.

---

[1]McKinney, Howard D. and W. R. Anderson, *Discovering Music*, American Book Co., New York, 1953.

Choir or *chorus* in elementary ...., junior high ....:, senior high ...., college ...., church ...., community ...., professional ....; part or voice ....; total years ....

Band in elementary ...., junior high ...., senior high ...., college ...., community ...., fraternal ...., professional ....; instrument or instruments ....; total years ....

Orchestra in elementary ...., junior high ...., senior high ...., college ...., community ...., professional ....; instrument or instruments ....; total years ....

List informal or recreational instruments you play ....

Do you now (N) or did you formerly (F) study:

Voice ....? Number of years of class study ....; private study?

Instruments (Name) ....? Years of class study ....; private study ....?

List the titles of any other music training classes you had in high school or college.

Indicate if you read music very little ...., some ...., quite well ...., or fluently ....

LISTENING EXPERIENCES

Indicate whether you listen to music on radio very little ...., some ...., quite a lot ...., or very frequently ....

If you have a FM radio, do you use it very little ...., some ...., quite a lot ...., very frequently ....?

If you own a phonograph, do you use it very little ...., some ...., quite a lot ...., or very frequently ....?

Do you have a record collection?

If you have a record collection, what percentage of your total collection would you classify as "classical" ....? Give the total number of records you have ....

Do you attend musical (ballet, chamber music, chorus, opera, solo recitals, symphony) programs seldom ...., some ...., quite often ...., very frequently ....?

How many concerts of this kind do you average in a month ....?

Do you read magazine articles, concert reviews, and books about music or recordings seldom ...., some ...., quite often ...., very frequently ....?

MUSIC PREFERENCES

Indicate by use of numbers (1, first choice; 2, second choice, etc.) your favorite instrumental or performing groups:
band ...., big dance band ...., chamber music ...., choir ...., concerti ...., small jazz combo ...., organ ...., piano ...., string orchestra ...., symphony ...., instrumental solo ...., western ...., novelty ...., folk singers ....
When buying records, what are your preferences? Use numbers.
Popular (including small jazz groups, dixieland, name bands, progressive jazz, vocalists, vocal combo) ....
Semi-classical (including light opera, show tunes, arrangements of operatic arias, dinner music, etc.) ....
Ethnic or *folk* ....
Classical (including keyboard instruments such as organ, piano, and harpsichord; symphonic music such as symphonies, suites, and concerti; chamber music such as sonatas, string quartets, etc.) ....

2. Let listeners initiate questions and meet their problems as they arise. Give them something to do and something to relate to in the music. This might start with stories, pictures, scrapbooks, ballet, drama, elements of music, or any specific background or interest of the group.
3. Involve individuals from the group as resource persons to gather and present information about the music, its composer, or the performing artists. Write pertinent data such as titles, composers, and dates on the chalk-board or have a complete listing of music to be used ready for distribution.
4. Plan long-range goals, but make each session of the group a complete, self-contained unit or installment so that newcomers can be absorbed into the group without too much repetition of materials.
5. Keep the format of the sessions flexible and use a variety of activities such as discussions, visual aids, and reviews of familiar music. Be ready and willing to alter the plan to fit the needs and moods of the group. Repeat music on request, or use the same melody in a different setting for variety's sake.
6. Be sure the listeners know the story behind the music. Relate the music to the listeners' previous experience by its instrumentation, its mood, its style, or its form, but set a time limit for these explanations and preliminaries. Too much talk is worse than none at all when music listening is the prime objective.

7. Play the music in its entirety, but keep it within the interest and attention spans of the listeners. Start with music that will catch the listeners' attention and at the same time set the mood or spirit for what is to follow. The period immediately after the opening selection is usually the time when interest and attention are best; this is the time to present the new, serious, or long work planned for this session. It may be that a small section, a movement, or selection from a larger work will suffice to introduce a major work and will be all that the group can absorb at the first hearing.

AUDIO EQUIPMENT

This entire listening program must be carried on within the limitations of time, budget, facilities, personnel, and other resources available. Suggestions for selection of audio equipment and recordings are available in current magazines, in library reference materials, in record catalogues, and from local dealers. There is no limit to the amount of money that can be spent on audio equipment, but one must try to secure the best equipment for the money he has to spend. Consideration should be given to how and where the audio equipment is to be used and what its most desirable and essential features are. For instance:

1. Is the equipment to be installed permanently or must it be portable?
2. Is the equipment easy to operate and to maintain?
3. Will instruction in operation and trained operators be available?
4. Will the equipment play all standard speed (33, 45, 78) recordings and can these speeds be altered for dance, swimming, or marching groups?
5. Can the equipment be used as a public address system and can instruction or calls be given along with the recorded music?
6. Are the fidelity and tone quality the best that can be had for the money available?
7. Are there separate bass and treble tone controls?

In situations where portability, ruggedness, and ease of operation are essential, it would be advisable to use monaural instead of stereophonic equipment and to use records instead of tapes; however, great strides are being made with stereophonic and taped sound, and both of these media should be considered in the light of budget and needs for the local situation. Stereophonic sound is not necessarily high-fidelity sound, and when a choice has to be made between the two, it usually is better to buy good, high-fidelity monaural equipment in preference to poorer, low-fidelity stereophonic equipment. Reserve expensive stereophonic equipment for use in the more formal listening situations, for stereophonic sound must be listened to with as much concentration and attention as one would give to an interesting telecast if one expected to derive the fullest benefit and enjoyment from it. The stereophonic effect is lost in casual situations where pople are talking or moving about. Good monaural equipment will suffice in most situations where background music is needed.

It is important that the elements of the sound system — the record player, amplifier, and speakers — be matched in quality, for a sound system is no better than its weakest component. Consider each of the elements of the audio system.

1. The motor of the record player must be powerful enough to turn records at a constant speed for all speed settings, and there must not be an appreciable "wow" or waver in the sound.
2. The record pick-up may contain a crystal, a ceramic, or a variable reluctance cartridge. The crystal pick-up is the cheapest available, and pick-ups progress from there in order of cost and desirability.
3. The wattage or output of the amplifier must be matched with the speaker system to give clear, undistorted audience coverage in a hall or in the out-of-doors.
4. The speaker or speakers must be correctly mounted and placed to give the best possible reproduction of the sound signal that comes to it. Up to a 12-inch speaker can be used with portable equipment, but larger speakers must be carefully installed to achieve the best results.

Once time, careful consideration, and money have been spent to acquire satisfactory audio equipment, it is essential that it be adequately housed, cared for, and kept in good working order. A trained crew of audio operators who know and enjoy their work can give and gain great satisfaction through their efforts, and at the same time help to keep maintenance bills at a minimum.

RECORD SELECTION AND CARE

A record selection committee to consult with and advise the recreation director should take responsibility for the choice of records. Consideration must be given to a variety of needs and tastes represented in the age and interest groups who will use the records. Band, orchestra, choral, solo, and novelty recordings all have a place in a balanced recreation library, but the number of each will depend upon local needs. A balanced distribution of record types for an average recreation center might include:

25% classical selections
10% semi-classical or show tunes
10% ethnic or folk music
15% folk or square dance
10% social dance
10% jazz
15% children's activity, rhythm, listening, or rest materials
 5% educational or literature recordings

One person should be given responsibility for ordering, receiving, inspecting, cataloguing, storing, and caring for records. Order records by correct title, recording company, and serial number; when recordings are received, inspect them carefully for needle drops, off-center pressings, warping, or gritty surfaces. They should be played and checked for incorrect labels or wrong sequences of music, bare spots, or insufficient stampings that would cause the needle to track incorrectly or to skip. A cataloguing or filing system can be developed, using cards for cross-indexing by titles, composers, artists, or performers for both sides of the records. Inclusion of sources of information about the music, the performers, how the recording can be used, or an analysis of record content on the filing card could be most helpful.

Store records vertically, on their edge, and in dust-proof jackets. Disc cabinets are available in seven, ten, twelve, or sixteen inch sizes to store 90 records in individual pockets. If the recreation music department is large enough, it should store all of its recordings in a central library. Duplicate copies of some of the most generally-used records would be necessary, and in some instances whole sets of recordings might be permanently assigned to an area recreation center for exclusive use there. It is essential that a close tab be kept on all records to avoid too much duplication or loss of equipment. All persons who handle recordings and recording equipment should be given these easy to follow rules:

1. Lift and hold records by their edges with fingers on the center label. Don't put finger marks on the grooves.
2. Wipe accumulated dust and lint from recordings with a lintless, damp cloth. Move the cloth with a circular motion in the same direction as the grooves.

3. Be sure to use the correct needle and motor speed specified for each record.
4. Turn down the volume before placing the pick-up needle on the record.
5. Turn down the volume before picking up the needle; lift the tone arm straight up and then move it to the side.
6. Avoid dropping the needle on the grooves.

SOME SUGGESTED LISTENING PROGRAMS

Familiar Classics

Generally speaking, one likes what he knows, and most listeners will be more receptive to new materials and new musical experiences if there is something familiar or if there is a relationship between the new music and things or situations already known. The link may be a recognized melody, a musical setting of a well-known poem or story, a tonal description of a geographical area or idea that is familiar to the listener, or a presentation of everyday experiences in a new setting.

Individuals who say they don't like "that classical stuff" may be amazed to discover how much fine classical music is already familiar to them, and that they or members of their families have been buying "pop" recordings of classical tunes without knowing the classic setting of the melodies they enjoy so much and so often. Here is a program of familiar melodies in their original setting or arrangement.

Espana Rhapsody	*Chabrier*
Symphony #5 in e minor Andante Cantabile	*Tschaikowsky*
Quartet #2 in D Scherzo and Notturno	*Borodin*
Piano Concerto #2 in c minor	*Rachmaninoff*
Quartet #1 in D Andante Cantabile	*Tschaikowsky*
Polonaise in A♭, Opus 53	*Chopin*
Pomp and Circumstance March	*Elgar*
Midsummer Nights Dream Wedding March	*Mendelssohn*

Program Music

Program music or music that suggests a story has the advantage of giving the listener an opportunity to relate music to an art or literature area in which he already has developed some familiarity and facility with the media of expression used. Some interesting possibilities for listening in this area include:

William Tell Overture...*Rossini*
    String basses and 'celli depict a sunrise in the Alps as an introduction for this beautiful tone painting. Then there is a raging storm with wind and rain; the storm dies away, a lovely solo for English horn accompanied by the flute expresses a shepherd's thanksgiving as he calls his scattered flock together again. This episode is followed by a stirring trumpet call; the marching music of the Swiss soldiers brings the overture to a rousing climax.

The Moldau...*Smetena*
    Smetena tells the story of a mighty river in this music. The river has its beginnings in two mountain streams that give rise to two interesting and contrasting themes or melodies. The streams join to form a mighty river which flows through the dark forest where the hunters' horns are heard in the distance. As it flows through the broad plain, the music of a peasant wedding is heard. Moonlight on the water, mighty castles, the clash of arms, rushing torrents, and finally the broad, majestic sweep of the river are suggested in this engaging music.

Dance Macabre...*Saint-Saens*
    A French poem that depicts the midnight frolicking of ghosts and skeletons is the basis for Saint-Saens' symphonic poem. Death tunes his three-stringed fiddle and specters dance to a waltz-like melody. At break of dawn a rooster's crow sends them all rushing back to their resting places.

The Sorcerer's Apprentice...*Dukas*
    While his master is away, a lazy apprentice uses the incantations he has heard to bring a broom to life. The broom is put to work carrying water, but the apprentice has forgotten the secret words that will break the spell. The room is soon flooded; the apprentice in his desperation chops the broom in half, and then the two halves resume the task of carrying the unwanted water. At last the master returns, and with a few chosen words he restores order.

Til Eulenspiegel...*R. Strauss*
    A series of episodes or "merry pranks" are described in this music. Our hero, Til, is pictured in the market place, as a priest,

as a lover, with the Philistines, in his struggles with himself, and finally in the last minutes before his death on the gallows.

The Fountains of Rome..*Respighi*

Respighi wrote that he "endeavored to give effect to the sentiment and vision suggested by four of Rome's fountains, contemplated at the hour at which their character is most in harmony with the surrounding landscape, and in which their beauty appears most impressive to the observer."

1. The Fountain at Valle Giulia, at Dawn
   "A pastoral landscape. Droves of cattle pass and disappear in the mists of a Roman Dawn."
2. The Fountain of the Tritons, in the Morning
   "A sudden loud and insistent blast of horns . . . is like a joyous call, summoning troops of Tritons and Naiads, who . . . pursue each other and mingle in the dance between the jets of water."
3. The Fountain of Trevi, at Noon
   "A solemn theme from the wood and brass assumes a triumphal character. Trumpets peal across the radiant surface of the water. Neptune's chariot passes, drawn by sea-horses and followed by Sirens and Tritons. The procession vanishes."
4. The Fountain of the Villa Medici, at Dusk
   "A sad theme rises above a subdued warbling. The air is full of tolling bells and birds twittering; then all dies peacefully in the silence of the night."

Carnival of the Animals..*Saint-Saens*

This series of short sketches originally was written as a musical joke. The sketches depict the sounds and the spirit of animals mentioned. The sections are called:

Introduction and Royal March of the Lion
Hens and Cocks
Wild Asses
Tortoises
The Elephant
Kangaroos
Aquarium
Personages with Long Ears
Cuckoo in the Woods
Birds

Fossils
The Swan
Pianists

Hary Janos Suite...*Kodaly*
The music from the suite is taken from Kodaly's folk opera of the same name. Some of the movements are highly descriptive and other sections are just good mood music; it all has to do with episodes in the life of Hary, the legendary, Hungarian folk hero, who might be compared to our American Paul Bunyan. Movements of the suite are titled:

1. Prelude, the Fairy Tale Begins
2. Viennese Musical Clock
3. Love Song
4. The Battle and Defeat of Napoleon
5. Intermezzo
6. Entrance of the Emperor and His Court

Instruments of the Orchestra

Instruments of the orchestra and band are of great interest to listeners irrespective of their age or their musical advancement. Practically all major recording companies have issued albums to demonstrate instruments individually or in combinations. Records of especial interest are:

Peter and the Wolf...*Prokofief*
The Man Who Invented Music..*Gillis*
Young Person's Guide to the Orchestra.............................*Britten*
First Chair..Columbia ML 4629
    Ormandy and the Philadelphia Orchestra
The Orchestra...Capitol SAL 8385
The Instruments of the Orchestra..............Vangaurd VRS 1017/8

Recordings designed to demonstrate instruments of the band and orchestra for children include:

Fun With Instruments.............................Victor   Y 467
The Hunter's Horn...................................Y. P. R.   421
The King's Trumpet ....Y. P. R.   5040
Licorice Stick ....Y. P. R.   420
Little Brass Band ....Y. P. R.   703
Rondo for Bassoon and Orchestra..............Y. P. R.   1009

Rusty in Orchestraville...Capitol   BC 35
Said the Piano to the Harpsichord.....................Y. P. R.   411
Tubby the Tuba ....Decca   CU 106
The Wonderful Violin ....Y. P. R.   311

Vocal Qualities

Women's voices generally are classified as soprano or alto while men's voices are either tenor or bass. These classifications are based upon the singer's vocal range: the classifications then can be categorized specifically as coloratura, lyric, dramatic or mezzo-soprano; mezzo or contralto alto; lyric or dramatic tenor; and baritone, contante, or profondo bass depending upon the range, quality, or style of singing involved. Recorded examples of each of these vocal classifications are listed in the standard music appreciation textbooks and in record catalogues. Rather than give a listing of songs or arias, it will suffice to suggest the name of recognized singers in each of the classifications or styles listed.

Coloratura soprano....Joan Sutherland, Lily Pons, Maria Callas
Lyric soprano............Ada Alsop, Dorothy Maynor, Frances Alda
Dramatic soprano......Helen Traubel, Eleanor Steber, Astrid Varnay
Mezzo-soprano ....Cleo Elmo, Gladys Swarthout, Rise Stevens
Contralto ....Bruna Castagna, Marian Anderson, Carol Brice
Lyric tenor...............Ferruccio Taglovini, Jussi Bjoerling
Dramatic tenor.........Karl Liebl, Lauritz Melchior
Baritone ....Tito Gobi, Leonard Warren, Robert Merrill
Basso contante.........Boris Christoff, Ezio Pinza, Alexander Kipnis

Design or Form of Music

Study of form, plan, or design in music leads to an understanding of the methods or plans composers use to organize their materials into significant musical expressions. In most instances the purpose or nature of the music determines and dictates its form. For example, (1) in a musical setting of a poem the repetition of a number of stanzas will extend a simple tune, and the return to a refrain or chorus will be used as a contrasting and unifying element; (2) various episodes or a series of events as they evolve in a story will dictate the form and design of the music the story suggests; (3) music that inspires or accompanies activities, such as work songs and dance routines, derives its form from the repetitive movements of the task or dance.

The suites of Bach and other composers of his time were collections of dances arranged in contrasting order of fast and slow tempi and in related keys; when suites were written and played as pure or absolute music for their own worth and beauty, the pattern and order of the early dance forms were retained.

Composers use repetition, variation, and contrast to extend musical compositions. Repetition gives emphasis to an idea, gives a feeling of order and unity, and fixes the idea firmly in the mind of the listener. Variation attempts to say the same thing or to express a musical idea in several different ways; this may be accomplished by change of words in a song, change of instruments, change of rhythm, or through melodic elaboration. Contrast is accomplished through use of another musical idea in relation to the first idea or theme presented. When repetition, variation, and contrast are used in a single, large composition, unity is developed by use of repetition, and variety is achieved by use of variation and contrast.

The use of variation (A, A^1, A^2, A^3, etc.) to extend a musical idea can be traced in these examples:

Passacaglia in c minor..*Bach*

Symphony No. 94 in G major (Surprise).....................*Haydn*
    Second movement — Andante

String Quartet in C major, Op. 76, No. 3.................*Haydn*
    (Emperor)
Second movement — Poco adagio cantabile

String Quartet in d minor, Op. 7, No. 3 (Death and
    the Maiden)..*Schubert*
    Second movement

Quintet in D major, Op. 114 (The Trout).....................*Schubert*

Symphony No. 5 in c minor, Op. 67.........................*Beethoven*
    Second movement — Andante con moto

Symphony No. 7 in A major...*Beethoven*
    Second movement — Allegretto

Symphony No. 4 in e minor, Op. 98.............................*Brahms*
    Finale

Symphonic Variations..*Franck*

Variations on a Theme of Tschaikowsky, Op. 35a........*Arensky*

Examples of extension by adding a contrasting idea (A, B) are found in musical literature. For instance, listen to:

Death and the Maiden, Op. 7, No. 3............................ *Schubert*
Waltzes, Op. 39, No. 3... *Brahms*
Prelude, Opus 28, No. 22... *Chopin*

Two-part form can be further extended by repeating the first section (A, B, A) after the second section.

Moment Musical No. 5 in f minor, Op. 94................. *Schubert*
Waltz in A♭ major, Op. 39, No. 15............................ *Brahms*
Schon Rosmarin... *Kreisler*

Another extension into a rondo form (A, B, A, C, A) is made through the introduction of additional contrasting material.

Nocturne, Op. 55, No. 1.. *Chopin*
Mazurka No. 33 in B major, Op. 56, No. 1................ *Chopin*
Nocturne from Midsummer Night's Dream.................. *Mendelssohn*

In each of these extended compositions, the ability to remember and to recognize the return of the original (A) melody should be developed for greater understanding and enjoyment of the music.

Each of the forms mentioned could stand alone as a complete and independent musical composition, but many times these forms that have been described and illustrated are joined together to constitute a bigger, more complex musical selection. The Intermezzo from the Hary Janos Suite of Kodaly is a good example of this extension of a musical work, and the entire Hary Janos Suite typifies the modern suite in contrast to the early dance suites previously mentioned. This suite was extracted from Kodaly's opera of the same name so that the various selections can be played independently of the larger operatic work. Similar suites have been drawn from Bizet's opera, Carmen, and while the separate units in the suite can be written as variations, two or three part compositions, or rondos, and can be played as independent, complete works, the composer has grouped the compositions together under a general subject heading or plot.

This idea of contrasting moods, tempi, and keys has been carried from the suite into the sonata, the concerto, and the symphony. Each of these works is made up of three or four movements in fast, slow, fast tempi and employs a variety of musical forms, depending upon the period in which the music was written.

Polyphonic or canonic forms comprise another large and general classification in the design or plan of musical compositions. The word polyphonic refers to a texture or style of musical writing in which two or more melodies are combined; contrasted to polyphony is monophonic music in which a single melodic line is supported by an harmonic or chordal background.   A whole series of treatments or procedures gives rise to many interesting polyphonic compositions such as the round, the canon, and the fugue which are repetitions of an original melody in different ways.   Some representative works on recordings include:

Round and Round..Y. P. R.   431
Fugue in g minor (The Little).....................................*Bach*

While contrapuntal style of writing reached its zenith in the composition of Bach, it still is used by contemporary composers.   Britten used a fugue as the climax to his set of variations in his Young Person's Guide to the Orchestra and Weinberger wrote a wonderful fugue in his opera Schwanda.

Religious Music

An interesting unit on religious music from many parts of the world would appeal to serious-minded listeners.   The recordings have an historical as well as a religious significance, and are examples of the splendid resources that are available in this fascinating study area.

Religious Music of India...Folkways
                                                                                       P 431

Band three is an example of Vedic chanting which is about three thousand years old.   The notation is by numbers so that chanting remains identical in all parts of India.

Band four is a Raga played on flutes.   When a religious ceremony is performed, the atmosphere must be purified by sounds from wind instruments and drums.   The orchestra is placed in front of the door to the ceremonial room and plays continuously.

Music of the Middle East — Palestine.....................Folkways
                                                                                       EFL 1408

Side A, Band 8: Bible Recitation (Leviticus 16-1) "And the Lord spoke unto Moses after the death of the two sons of Aaron, when they offered before the Lord and died."

The Middle Eastern musician must confine himself to themes well-known to his audience.   This music is not written but is taught person to person, from mouth to ear.

Masterpieces of Music Before 1750.............................Haydn Society
                                                                                       HSL 2071

Antiphon; Laus Deo Patri

Music of the World's People...................................Folkways
P 504
Band thirteen — A "Lament for the Dead" from Tibet has been used by the Lamas for many centuries.

Masterpieces of Music Before 1750.........................Haydn Society
HSL 2071
Band six — Parallel Organum, Sequence: Rex caeli, Domine from the ninth century.
Band seven — Free Organum, Trope: Agnus Dei from the twelfth century.

Twelfth and Thirteenth Century Music...................EMS 201
Band two — Deum Time from the middle of the twelfth century.

Music of the World's People...................................Folkways
P 504

Band three

This style of spontaneous part singing is a very prevalent part of the service for the contemporary Greek Orthodox Church in Caucasian countries.

Masterpieces of Music Before 1750.........................Haydn Society
HSL 2071
Side two, band thirteen — Mass: Notre Dame by Machaut (1300-1377) is given as the first setting of the Mass by one composer.
Side two, band two — Mass for Pope Marcelli by Palestrina (1526-1594) was written at the request of the eight cardinals appointed by the Council of Trent in 1562 as a model for the music desired in the Catholic service.

Bach's Royal Instrument.......................................Columbia
E. Power Biggs, organist
The choral melody, Sleepers Awake, is played in a four-part harmonization and then as a Choral Prelude, both settings by Bach.

The Messiah ....Handel
(1685-1759)
Choruses from this magnificent work will serve to illustrate how far the composers of religious music had come by the eighteenth century.

Music of the World's People...................................Folkways
P 504

Band sixteen — A contemporary example from Spain shows a mixture of Moorish and European elements in the canto hondo or deep song.

Belshazzar's Feast by William Walton (1902)............Westminster
                                                       WL 5248

This colossal work for band, orchestra, and chorus was first performed in 1931 and is an outstanding example of a contemporary setting for a Bible story.

Music for Holy Days
Christmas

Christmas Hymns...Robert Shaw Chorale
    Volume I RCA Victor   LM 1711
    Volume II RCA Victor   LM 2139

Christmas Around the World.................................Svend Soaby Choir

To Wish You a Merry Christmas.......................Harry Belafonte
    R C A Victor   LPM 1887

Songs of Christmas..Norman Luboff Choir
    Columbia   CL 926

The Littlest Angel..Loretta Young
    Decca   DLP 8009

Concerto Grosso No. 8 in g minor (Christmas)..Corelli

Joy To The World...Robert Wagner Chorale
    Capitol   P 8353

Little Bitty Baby
    Young People's Records   YPR 225

Easter

Russian Easter Overture.......................................Rimsky-Korsakoff

Excerpts from the Easter Oratorio......................Bach
    Vangaurd-Bach Guild   BG 507
        Side one, bands one, two, and three

Prelude and Good Friday Spell (Parsifal).......Wagner
    Urania   URLP 7065

Easter Songs..Robert Shaw Chorale
    RCA Victor   LM 1201

Composers of Our United States

Symphonic Sketches..*Chadwick*
    Mercury   MG 50104

Adagio for Strings..*Barber*
    Capitol   SAL 8385

The White Peacock..*Griffes*
    Mercury   MG 50085

Memories of My Childhood..*Loeffler*
    Mercury   MG 50085

Second "Indian" Suite..*MacDowell*
    Mercury   MG 50082

Through the Looking Glass..*Taylor*
    Mercury   MG 50081

Merrymount Suite..*Hanson*
    Mercury   MG 50175

Music for and About Children

Children's Corner Suite..*Debussy*
    Columbia   ML 4539; Walter Giesiking, Pianist

Scenes from Childhood..*Schuman*
    Columbia   ML 4540; Walter Giesiking, Pianist

Suite from Childhood..*H. McDonald*
    RCA Victor   DM 754

Happy Instruments..*Kleinsinger*
    Columbia   CL 1026

This Is Jazz!

On Jazz..*Leonard Bernstein*
    Columbia   CL 918

The Story of Jazz
    Folkways   FJ 7312

Art Tatum, Trio (Rehearsal)
    Folkways   FJ 2293

Encyclopedia of Jazz
    Decca   DX 140

History of Jazz
    Capitol   T 793-796

Chamber Music

Quartet in F Major, Op. 3, No. 5...*Haydn*
Quintet for Clarinet and Strings   K. 581...............................*Mozart*
Quintet in E♭ major, Op. 44 (Piano)......................................*Schumann*
Quartet in g minor...*Debussy*

Interesting and varied programs could be built around:

a. Keyboard music
b. Folk music
c. Music for strings
d. A night at the opera
e. Art songs
f. Music to accompany Shakespeare
g. Dance music then and now
h. The contemporary music
i. The band's music
j. Solo literature
k. Musical personalities
l. Great performances
m. Onomatopoetic music
n. Literature and music

Call upon specialists for help in building programs. Amateur or professional musicians, librarians in school or public libraries, or salespeople in record shops usually are happy to be of assistance when music and recordings are involved. Many current magazines feature record reviews and make program suggestions for different listening situations.

TOPICS FOR DISCUSSION AND ASSIGNMENT
Listening

1. List as many concert artists as you can.   Include vocalists, pianists, other instrumentalists, and conductors.   Underscore the names of artists you have seen and heard in person.
2. How many local civic musical organizations can you list?   Can you name the directors of these groups?
3. Develop a scrapbook of your listening and concert-going activities.
4. Build a file of materials such as catalogues, pictures, record lists, programs, etc. for use in the listening area.
5. Start a personal record collection.

6. Organize a half-hour "name that tune" program for use in a recreational situation.
7. Prepare a one-page, written report on your favorite composer. Program a half-hour listening program of his compositions.
8. Develop evaluation forms for a recreational listening program from the standpoint of the leader and from the standpoint of the listener.
9. Plan and create a bulletin board featuring music listening for recreation.
10. Read and report from books and magazine articles about music listening for recreation.

BIBLIOGRAPHY FOR MUSIC LISTENING

Paul Affelder
How to Build a Record Library
Dutton & Co., New York, N. Y., 1947
Lillian Baldwin
A Listener's Anthology of Music
Silver-Burdett, New York, N. Y., 1948
Lillian Baldwin
Music to Remember: A Book for Listeners
Silver-Burdett, New York, N. Y., 1951
John D. Ball
Records for Pleasure
Rutgers University Press, New Brunswick, New Jersey, 1947
Jacques Barzun
Pleasures of Music
Viking Press, New York, N. Y., 1951
Leonard Bernstein
The Joy of Music
Simon & Schuster, New York, N. Y., 1959
Aaron Copland
Our New Music
Whittlesey House, New York, N. Y., 1948
Leon Dallin
Listener's Guide to Musical Understanding
Wm. C. Brown Company Publishers, Dubuque, Iowa, 1959
Leonard Feather
The Encyclopedia Yearbook of Jazz
Horizon Press, New York, N. Y., 1960

William L. Grossman and Jack W. Farrell
    The Heart of Jazz
        University Press, New York, N. Y., 1956
John Tasker Howard
    Our American Music
        Thomas Y. Crowell & Co., New York, N. Y., 1954
Robert Jacobs
    Harmony for the Listener
        Oxford University Press, New York, N. Y., 1958
Irvine Kolodin
    New Guide to Recorded Music
        Doubleday, New York, N. Y., 1950
Stephen Longstreet
    The Real Jazz Old and New
        Louisiana State University, Baton Rouge, La., 1956
Joseph Machlis
    The Enjoyment of Music
        W. W. Norton & Co., Inc., New York, N. Y., 1955
Howard McKinney and W. D. Anderson
    Discovering Music
        American Book Co., New York, N. Y., 1953
Howard A. Murphy
    Form in Music for the Listener
        Radio Corporation of America, Camden, N. J., 1948
Hugues Panassie
  A Guide to Jazz
        Houghton Mifflin, Boston, Mass., 1956
Curt Sachs
    A History of Musical Instruments
        W. W. Norton & Co., New York, N. Y., 1940
Percy Scholes
    The Listeners Guide to Music
        Oxford University Press, New York, N. Y., 1942
Marshall Stearns
    The Story of Jazz
        Oxford University Press, New York, N. Y., 1956
Edwin Stringham
    Listening to Music Creatively
        Prentice-Hall, New York, N. Y., 1946
Howard Taubman
  How to Build a Record Library
        Hanover House, Garden City, N. Y., 1953

Howard Taubman
    How to Bring up Your Child to Enjoy Music
        Doubleday & Co., New York, N. Y., 1958
Augustus Zanzig
    Roads to Music Appreciation
        National Recreation Association, New York, N. Y., 1948

CHILDREN'S BOOKS

Jan Balet
    What Makes an Orchestra?
        Oxford University Press, New York, N. Y., 1951
Harriet Buxton Barbour and Warren S. Freeman
    Children's Record Book
        Oliver Durrell, Inc., New York, N. Y., 1947
Donzella Cross
    Music Stories for Boys and Girls
        Ginn & Co., Boston, Mass., 1926
Philip Eisenberg and Hecky Kracy
    A Guide to Children's Records
        Crown Publishers, New York, N. Y., 1948
Harriet Huntington
    Tune-Up
        Doubleday & Co., Inc., Garden City, N. Y., 1942

CHAPTER 6

Community, Recreational Services

Persons interested in recreation must constantly build public awareness of community needs in recreation; we must help others to develop a broadened concept of what is included in an adequate recreation program and what segments of the total population the program should reach. Specialists in recreation administration will establish policies as to the activities to sponsor, the budget and equipment to implement these activities, and the motivation and leadership to keep the activities moving in the right direction once they have been started. It is essential that other community agencies be made a part of the program in order to bring about joint use of public facilities and utilization of potential community leadership.

The school department, adult education program, churches, service clubs, and youth groups should be involved in helping, educating, and training the public to make sound value judgments in their choice of recreation activities, in developing the family as a recreation unit, and in teaching recreation skills that can be utilized in the home.

One of the finest means of coordinating the efforts of existing groups to promote recreation music is to form a community committee to do basic planning, to utilize leadership skills, to insure complete coverage of the entire community, and to avoid duplication of effort and facilities. A representative group from the entire community should develop a master calendar to include all cultural events in its immediate area and to publicize these events; it also should conduct surveys of local needs and resources in a given situation.

The recreation department should supply a variety of services to its clients in the community. For instance, it might:

1. Maintain a storage area and clearing house for the care, maintenance, and distribution of musical instruments, audio equipment, records, tapes, and film. The function of getting the right equipment to the right place at the right time could be a most important link in a vital and interesting recreation program. A competent technician should be employed for a regular semiannual inspection and tuning of all pianos used in the department.

2. Provide an adequate library of books, materials, and supplies that are recommended and available to persons in recreation or allied work. Sample or demonstration kits of these materials could be circulated among interested personnel.

3. Publicize recreation and entertainment events available to the community. For musical activities this should include information about radio, television, or live concerts sponsored by school, church, or other cultural groups. Bulletins, bulletin boards, newspaper articles, announcements, or word-of-mouth publicity can do much to stimulate interest.

4. Act as an organizational center to bring persons of like interests together to share their information and their company. The provision of a schedule of events and a place to meet may become one of the most rewarding services that the recreation leader can furnish for his community.

The recreation department, alone or in conjunction with other community agencies, can initiate, sponsor, and support music instruction and performance in the community. Vocal and instrumental groups or solosists from schools, churches, or other sources can be encouraged to perform individually or as combined organizations.

Vocal festivals for soloists or for groups in which performers sing for each other and receive comments, suggestions, and criticisms from a capable adjudicator or clinician can be sponsored by the recreation department. Novelty or barbershop groups, a name artist, or a well-known personality can help to spark interest and draw a good audience.

Similar festivals featuring instrumental soloists or groups can include bands, orchestras, chamber ensembles, jazz combinations, drum and bugle corps, marching units, unusual instruments or unusual groupings of instruments such as accordions, harmonicas, mandolins, guitars, fiddle, folk, or homemade instruments that are not usually found in the concert band or symphony orchestra. The entire area of folk instruments and folk dances could provide motivation for many interesting programs.

Vocal and instrumental groups can be brought together in massed festival or honor organizations for special occasions. These activities afford musicians opportunities to perform the finest literature under capable and distinguished leadership, to become acquainted with new program materials, to learn new rehearsal and performance techniques, to provide incentive and motivation for the participants, and to present enjoyable and entertaining programs in the communities involved. Once a concert of this kind has been organized for performance, it can be repeated in other areas in the community from which the individual participants come.

All of these activities should take place throughout the entire year, but they become especially important during the holiday season and during the summer when the schools are not in session. The school music teachers or supervisors could be hired to hold regular rehearsals for school groups during summer vacations. In many instances entire families would be eligible for participation in these activities. Such groups might give a series of public outdoor concerts, or their summer activities might culminate with a massed concert. A picked band made up of selected players from the area might become the official city, recreation, or school department band to appear and represent their city in parades and other civic functions in their own and in neighboring communities during the summer or at other times when schools are on vacation.

MUSICAL TALENT AND VARIETY SHOWS

Often the recreation leader is called upon to sponsor, organize, or direct talent and variety shows. This involves exploration of talent that is available, facilities and equipment necessary to stage a show, and possible themes around which a show can be structured. Once the theme and the objectives for staging the show have been established, a time and place for auditions or try-outs for participation in the show must be arranged. In most instances it is a good idea to form a committee to share responsibility and to utilize opinions of experts in the entertainment areas that will be involved. Each person or group that expects to try out for the show should supply the following information:

1. Names of all performers in the act.
2. What they expect to do.

3. How long their performance will take.
4. Special equipment needed in their performance.
   a. Do they have their own accompanist?
   b. Do they have their own music?
   c. If recordings are to be used, are they in good condition and playable on the phonograph that is available?
   d. Can they perform in the space available?

Insist upon auditioning every performing group before it is scheduled on the program and reserve the right to limit the time on stage that any act will take.

Rehearse each act or unit of the show singly; there is no reason all the performers be present while the other acts practice their routines. If there are parts of the show that will involve all of the performers at the same time, schedule this early in the rehearsal time and then release the performers as soon as their part of the show has been practiced. Rehearsals should establish the routine for each performer. This will include the time and place in the show when the performer will appear; how he will be announced; how he will get on and off the performing area; the sequence of numbers in each act; and finally the routine and procedures in case of an encore. Check all music and equipment to be used in each act and make someone personally responsible for these properties at the time of the performance. The importance of a capable pianist as an accompanist cannot be overemphasized. Set tempi by having the performer do part of his number as he wants it; then a good accompanist will pick up the tempo from the performer.

Keep these factors in mind while establishing the sequence of acts in the show:

1. There must be a good, flashy performance to start the program and catch audience attention.
2. Serious numbers or acts requiring concentration should be programmed early in the show while audience attention is at its best.
3. The show must move quickly and build toward a climax.
4. The next to last spot on the program usually is reserved for the best or "headline" act.
5. If it is at all possible, bring the entire company back for the finale of the show even if it is for just a bow.
6. It is better to have an outstanding, short show than one that is too long. The audience should leave while wishing for more!

7. Often the show can be tied together by a capable master of ceremonies, but he must know what the show is about, the correct pronunciation of all names in his script, and what his functions are in the show.

Once the program numbers have been arranged, an organization must be formed to see that there is a show and that there is an audience. Involve as many people as possible in this process, but make specific individuals responsible for specific duties or functions so there will be no overlapping of effort or conflict of interests. Try to give definite instructions as to what is to be done and who has the responsibility for its performance in each instance. People who are asked to do a job should know what moneys are available to them and who has the power to authorize their expenditure.

Conductor's books for band shows published for use at football games suggest some useful themes for variety shows. Ideas that were mentioned for listening and singing sessions, such as holiday, seasonal, or folk themes, could be developed into a successful variety show. Community singing or a "Name That Tune" session can provide for audience participation. Standard operettas or current musical shows often will suggest a usable theme, but be sure to investigate performance rights, restrictions, and fees before going too far in this area. Generally, a show that becomes this elaborate will entail use of professional direction of music and of staging.

Displays of musical collections such as sheet music, phonograph records, old instruments or phonographs, scrapbooks, or pictures might be an interesting part of a hobby show, and amateur groups can be invited to play as a part of the hobby show program. Possibilities for combining music with other recreation activities have been discussed in other sections of this book.

Finally, let it be suggested again that the recreation leader need not have all the musical skills mentioned in this book in order to carry on a successful recreation music program. There are many effective resources in the form of books and records that are practically self-explanatory in all of the areas of music participation that have been suggested. For the recreation leader, as for his clients, the accumulation of skills brings the ability to participate in new activities and opens new avenues for adventure. Motivation is sustained through new understandings, and new understanding can come only through experience and new exposure. Start with familiar activities that involve the ear and ability to listen efficiently; this can be just listening, in physical or rhythmic response to music, in singing, or in playing musical instruments, but the ability to hear and to remember what has been heard are the fundamental bases for the understanding and enjoyment of music.

BIBLIOGRAPHY FOR GENERAL MUSIC AND RECREATION

Activities for Rainy Days. Prepared by the Tennessee State Committee of the Cooperative Program in Elementary Education sponsored by the Southern Association of Colleges and Secondary Schools. Nashville 3, Tennessee: Tennessee State Department of Education, 1955. (Multilithed from typewritten copy, 104 pp.)

Fred Barton. *Music as a Hobby.* New York: Harper & Sons, 1950.

B. A. Botkin. *A Treasury of American Folklore.* New York: Crown Publishers, 1944.

Ethel Bowers. *Parties, Plans, and Programs.* New York: National Recreation Association, 1950.

Gerald P. Burns. *Program of the Modern Camp.* New York: Prentice-Hall, Inc., 1954.

George D. Butler. *Introduction to Community Recreation.* New York: National Recreation Association, 1940.

Madeleine Carbo-Cone & Beatrice Royt. *How to Help Children Learn Music.* New York: Harper Bros., 1960.

Madeleine Carbo-Cone. *The Playground as a Music Teacher,* New York: Harper Bros., 1960.

Davis Champlin. *Music and the Child.* New York: Child Study Association of America, 1930.

Dan Corbin. *Recreational Leadership.* New York: Prentice-Hall, 1953.

Howard G. Danford. *Recreation in the American Community.* New York: Harper, 1953.

Clement A. Duran. *The Program Encyclopedia.* New York: Association Press, 1955.

Helen & Larry Eisenberg. *Omnibus of Fun.* New York: Association Press, 1956.

Lehman Engel. *Planning and Producing the Musical Show.* New York: Crown Publishers, Inc., 1958.

Alex Field. *Novelty Dances for Any Operetta.* New York: Music Publishers Holding Company, 1954.

Marion Flagg. *Musical Learning: A Guide to Child Growth.* Boston: C. C. Birchard, 1949.

Ella Gardner. "Handbook for Recreation Leaders." Federal Security Agency, U. S. Government Printing Office, Publication 231. Washington, D. C., 1948.

Inez Homewood. *Music in Further Education.* London: Dennis Dobson, Ltd., 1951.

Charles T. Jones & Don Wilson. *More Power to the Showman.* New York: Music Publishers Holding Company, 1954.

Marion Jordalen & Alice J. Eppink. The Who, What and Where Music Series, Book I. *Musicians.* A Listing of Films, Books, Pictures on People in Music, Compiled Expressly for the Classroom Teacher of Music. San Francisco 14: Library Music Services (4107–17 St.), 1954 (multilithed).

Thomas Koskey, *Baited Bulletin Boards.* San Francisco, California: Fearon Press, 1955.

Richard G. Krauss. *Recreation Leader's Handbook.* New York: McGraw-Hill, 1955.

Beatrice Krone. *Music Participation in Elementary Schools.* Chicago, Illinois: Kjos, 1952.

Beatrice Krone, and Kurt Miller. *Help Yourselves to Music,* San Francisco, California: Howard Chandler, 1959.

Charles Leonhard. *Recreation Through Music.* New York: Barnes, 1952.

L. Eileen McMillan. *Guiding Children's Growth Through Music.* Boston: Ginn and Co., 1959.

National Recreation Association. *Recreation Activities for Adults.* New York: Association Press, 1950.

Gertrude Norman. *The First Book of Music.* New York: F. Watts, 1954.

Robert E. Nye & Bjornar Bergethon. *Basic Music for Classroom Teachers.* New York: Prentice-Hall, Inc., 1954.

Robert E. Nye & Vernice Nye. *Music in the Elementary Schools,* New York: Prentice-Hall, 1957.

Cornelia Parker. *Your Child Can Be Happy in Bed.* New York: Crowell Company, 1952.

Emma Sheehy. *There's Music in Children.* New York: Holt & Co., 1946.

Alice M. Snyder. *Creating Music With Children.* New York: Mills Music Co., 1957.

Sigmund Spaeth. *Music for Fun.* Philadelphia: Blakesgon Co., 1939.

William R. Sur and Charles F. Schuller. *Music Education for Teenagers,* New York: Harper Bros., 1958.

Jane E. Tobitt. *ABC's of Camp Music.* New York: Plymouth Music Co., 1955.

BIBLIOGRAPHY FOR MUSIC THERAPY, MUSIC IN INDUSTRY, AND MUSIC FOR THE AGED

Kenneth S. Clark
  Music In Industry
    National Bureau for the Advancement of Music, New York, 1929
John Davis
  Clinical Applications of Recreational Therapy
    Chas. Thomas, Springfield, Ill., 1950
Esther G. Gilliland
  Music Therapy, 1952
    National Association for Music Therapy
      Allen Press, Lawrence, Kansas, 1953
Susan H. Kubic and Gertrude Londau
  Group Work with the Aged
    International Universities, New York, 1953
Sidney Licht
  Music in Medicine
    New England Conservatory of Music, Boston, 1946
Leonard B. Meyer
  Emotion and Meaning in Music
    University of Chicago Press, Chicago, 1956
National Association for Music Therapy
  Music Therapy, 1953
    Third Book of Proceedings of the National Association for Music Therapy
      Allen Press, Lawrence, Kansas, 1953
Max Schoen (ed.)
  Effects of Music — a series of essays
    Harcourt Brace, New York, 1927
Dorothy May Schullian and Max Schoen
  Music and Medicine
    Henry Schuman, Inc., New York, 1948
Doris Soibelman
  Theraputic and Industrial Uses of Music
    Columbia University Press, New York, 1948
Willem van de Wall
  Music in Hospitals
    Russell Sage Foundation, New York, 1946
Arthur Williams
  Recreation for the Aging
    National Recreation Association, New York, 1953

APPENDIX I

Rudiments of Music

Music is notated on a series of lines and spaces known as a staff. A grand staff has eleven lines and the resultant ten spaces between the lines. The lines and spaces can be compared to eleven strings on a harp or lute, and placement of notes on these lines or spaces indicates graphically the relative highness or lowness of pitches to be sounded.

These eleven lines and ten spaces are named for the first seven letters of the alphabet. The middle line or string (dotted line) of the grand staff is designated as middle C; it has a staff of five lines above it and a staff of five lines below it. The five lines above middle C are known as the treble or G clef, and a sign is placed at the start of this staff to locate the position of G on the second line of the treble staff.

Notice the similarity between this G clef sign and a written capital G (𝒢) and the fact that the loop at the bottom of the clef sign finishes or ends on the second line of the staff, which is named G in this treble clef.

The five lines below middle C are the bass or F clef, and a clef sign is placed at the start of this staff to locate the position of F on the fourth line of the bass staff.

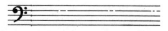

Notice the similarity between the F clef sign and a written F (𝒇) and the fact that the two dots-locate the position of F on the fourth line of the bass clef.

To name the lines in treble clef, start with E on the bottom line and fill in the letter names using the first seven letters of the alphabet.

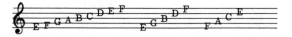

The lines are E, G, B, D, and F; between these are the spaces F, A, C, and E.

To name the lines and spaces in bass clef, start from G on the bottom line and fill in the names using the first seven letters of the alphabet.

The lines in bass clef are G, B, D, F, and A; between these are the spaces A, C, E, and G.

Additional lines and spaces, called ledger lines, can be added below or above the bass or treble staffs to indicate pitches higher or lower than those represented on the regular staff. These follow the same alphabetical pattern as those in the staff.

To relate these letter names to the piano keyboard, notice that the black keys on piano are arranged in groups of twos or threes.

The white key to the left of any group of two black keys is C; the white key to the left of the group of three black keys is F. Each white key up or down from C is a letter name located on the staff.

The usual letter names of pitches can be altered by the use of sharps (♯) which raise the pitch of any natural pitch to the next nearest pitch or key above on the piano keyboard, or by the use of flats (♭) which lower the pitch of any natural note to the next nearest pitch or key below on the piano. These alterations are known as accidentals and the distance or interval of alteration is a half-step, the next nearest pitch or key upward or downward on the piano keyboard, from any given letter name. Each alphabetical letter name has at least two possible alterations from its natural position. For instance, C may appear as a C natural (♮), C sharp (♯), or C flat (♭), depending upon the accidental or alteration placed before it.

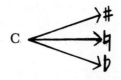

When the letter names appear without alteration, they are in their natural form and usually are played as the white keys on the piano keyboard. The five black keys in each octave of the piano are used to indicate an altered pitch. The name by which these alterations are designated depends upon the direction of the alteration. Since there are seven letter names involved in an octave, and each of these letter names has at least two alterations possible, it becomes evident that each of the black keys must serve for more than one pitch alteration. These keys or pitches that have the same sound but have different names are called enharmonic pitches, and those most frequently used are:

C♯ Db	D♯ Eb		F♯ Gb	G♯ Ab	A♯ Bb		C♯ Db
C	D	E	F	G	A	B	C

The pitch alteration usually is named in relation to the key in which it appears and to the direction from which it is approached. As the pitches ascend they are called by their sharp names (C♯, D♯, F♯, G♯, A♯); when the pitches descend, they are called by their flat names (B♭, A♭, G♭, E♭, D♭).

In most instances, the composer or arranger will place the alterations or accidentals belonging to the key or scale in which he is writing, on the staff to the right of the clef sign at the start of each line of the composition. These alterations define the key, pitch, and starting point for the composition. No key signature, that is no sharps or flats to the right of the clef sign, indicates the key of C so long as the music is in a major key.

To find the name of the major key when there are sharps in the key signature, take the sharp farthest to the right, call it seven of the scale, and count up to eight for the key name. For example, if the last sharp to the right in the key signature is C♯, the key is D major.

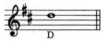

To find the name of the major key when there are flats in the key signature, take the flat farthest to the right, call it four and count down to one for the key name. For example, if the last flat to the right is B♭, the key is F major. When there is more than one flat in the key signature, the next to the last flat will indicate the key name.

The order of sharps or flats contained in the key signature can be memorized by use of the series:

♯ → Father Charles Goes Down And Ends Battle ← ♭

Reading from left to right the capitalized letters give the order of sharps in the key signature. If there is one sharp, it is always F sharp.

If there are two sharps, they are F sharp and C sharp and so on through the seven possible sharp alterations.

Notice that sharps are placed within the staff in order from left to right as they appear in the "Father Charles" series and that the F♯ is placed on the top line.

Reading from right to left, the capitalized letters give the order of flats in a key signature. If there is one flat, it is always B flat. If there are two flats, they are always B flat and E flat.

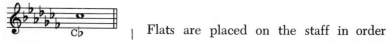 Flats are placed on the staff in order from right to left as they appear in the "Battle Ends" series. The B♭ is placed on the middle line and the order proceeds from low to high to low and so on. The first note to be sharped is the last note to be flatted, and the first note to be flatted is the last note to be sharped.

The appearance of sharps or flats in the key signature alters all of the notes called by that name which occur in the following composition whether the notes appear in, above, or below the staff, unless they are countermanded or changed by accidentals or alterations in the music. Any alterations from the key signature indicated by accidentals are valid for the entire measure in which they occur, unless they are cancelled or countermanded by other accidentals within that same measure. Exceptions to this rule occur when a pitch altered by an accidental is carried into the succeeding measures by a curved line known as a tie. Here the alteration is carried into the new measure or until it is cancelled by another accidental.

Using the order of sharps and flats and the rules for finding the key name when a signature is given, it is possible to construct a table or chart of the major keys involving sharps or flats.

Major Sharp Keys → G   D   A   E   B   F♯   C♯
Order of Sharps   → F   C   G   D   A   E   B   ←   Order of Flats
                     C♭ G♭ D♭ A♭ E♭ B♭   F   ←   Major Flat Keys

Thus for the scale or key of F♯ major which is listed in the top line, read from left to right in the middle line and sharp the pitches F, C, G, D, A, and E in that order when writing the key signature.

For flat keys read from right to left. The names of the flat keys or scales are found in the bottom line, and the names of the pitches to be altered will be found by reading from right to left in the middle line. For instance, if the key is G♭ major, the pitches altered will be B♭, E♭, A♭, D♭, G♭, and C♭, and they will appear in that order in the key signature.

Three other names or terms of identification are commonly used in musical nomenclature in addition to the letter names. These include syllable names, numerical names, and harmonic names. For example, the starting note of any major scale can be identified as doh, as one, or as the tonic in addition to its letter name.

F	G	A	B♭	C	D	E	F
doh	re	mi	fah	sol	la	ti	do
1	2	3	4	5	6	7	8
Tonic	Super-tonic	Mediant	Sub-dominant	Dominant	Sub-mediant	Leading tone	Tonic

As the major key changes, the new scale gets its letter name from, and is called by, the pitch on which the scale starts.

Each major scale has a related minor scale which has the same key signature as the major scale, but instead of starting the scale on doh as in the major key, the minor scale starts on lah or six of the major scale. Lah becomes one, or the tonic, in the minor keys, and the minor scale takes its letter name from the note on which it starts.

There is a quick method of finding the related minor key. If the major scale name is on a line in the staff, the related minor scale will start on and will be named for the next line below; if the major scale letter name is on a space, the related minor scale will be named for the next space below. Be sure to refer to the key signature in each instance and be cognizant of any alterations of the letter names in the minor scale. Minor keys and chords are usually designated by lower case or small letters; major keys and chords are designated by capital or large letters.

The "Father Charles" table of keys can be expanded to include minor along with major keys.

Minor sharp keys → e b f♯ c♯ g♯ d♯ a♯
Major sharp keys → G D A E B F♯ C♯
Order of sharps → F C G D A E B ← Order of flats
                       C♭ G♭ D♭ A♭ E♭ B♭ F ← Major flat keys
                       a♭ e♭ b♭ f c g d ← Minor flat keys

The key of C major and its related minor (a) are not shown on the table. Notice that the first note of the minor scale is called one and is the tonic, but its syllable name is lah.

There are three forms of the minor scale. The natural or pure form conforms to the written key signature both ascending and descending; the harmonic form differs from the natural by having the seventh degree of the scale raised a half step both ascending and descending; the melodic form differs from the natural form by having both the sixth and seventh degrees of the scale raised a half step as it ascends and then conforming to the key signature (natural form) as it descends. The harmonic form, as its name implies, is used for chording. The three primary chords are built on the first (tonic), fourth (subdominant), and fifth (dominant) degrees of the scale, and the raised seventh of the scale is an important component of the dominant chord. For example, F major and f minor have the same dominant seventh chord, although the F major has one flat and f minor has four flats.

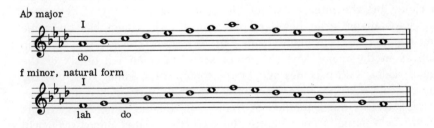

A♭ major

f minor, natural form

f minor, harmonic form

f minor, melodic form

RHYTHMIC NOTATION

Whole, half, quarter, eighth, and sixteenth notes and their equivalent rests are used to indicate duration or value of pitches or rests in this book.

NOTES	NAMES	RESTS
o	Whole	▬
♩	Half	▬
♩	Quarter	𝄽
♪	Eighth	𝄾
♬	Sixteenth	𝄿

Notice that each addition to the whole note cuts its value in half. (The addition of the stem to the whole note makes it a half note; filling in the body of the half note reduces it to a quarter note, etc.)

The actual duration of notes or rests is determined by the meter signature and by the tempo or speed of the music. The meter signature appears just after the key signature at the start of a musical composition, and tempo indications usually are placed just above the key and meter signatures.

Moderato

Generally speaking the upper number in the meter signature indicates the number of beats or pulses in a measure, while the lower number identifies the kind of note that receives one beat or pulse. For example:

3 = beats in each measure
4 = each quarter note or its equivalent is given one beat

These are only general statements and experienced musicians can cite many exceptions. Two symbols commonly used in place of the numbers for meter signatures are:

C to indicate $\frac{4}{4}$ meter

¢ to indicate "Alla breve" or $\frac{2}{2}$ meter.

Duration of notes can be increased by tying notes together(𝅗𝅥‿𝅗𝅥) or by using dots immediately after the notes (𝅗𝅥.). The dot after a note increases the value of the note by one-half its original value. In 6—4 meter these values can be notated:

𝅝‿𝅗𝅥 or 𝅝.   = 4+2 or 6 beats

𝅘𝅥‿𝅘𝅥 or 𝅘𝅥.   = 2+1 or 3 beats

𝅘𝅥‿𝅘𝅥𝅮 or 𝅘𝅥.   = 1+ 1/2 or 1 1/2 beats

RHYTHM CHART

1. Establish a steady beat by clapping the hands or tapping the right foot. In any meter in which the quarter note is the one beat unit (2-4, 3-4, 4-4, etc.) play or sing a quarter note on each down beat of the hand or foot. Say the symbol "down" for each note (D for down) when it is to be played or sung.

Example: $\frac{4}{4}$ D D D D | D D D D | D D D D

2. To play or sing eighth notes in any meter where the quarter note is the one beat unit, divide the established beat into two equal parts, a down half and an up half, and play or sing an eighth note on each part of the beat, one on the down, one on the up (D for down, U for up). Be sure to keep a steady four beat.

Example:

3. Combinations of quarter and eighth notes are said at the exact time when they are to be played or sung and are held or sustained until the next note or rest occurs. Keep a steady beat.

Examples:

3a.

3b.

3c.

4. Two sixteenth notes are played or sung on each part of the divided beat, two on the down beat and two on the up beat. Say 1-2 on the down beat and 1-2 on the up beat.

Examples:

4a.

4b.

5. Combinations of sixteenth and eighth notes are grouped within the steady beat. Each of the examples is grouped in a one beat pattern.

Examples:

5a. $\frac{4}{4}$ 1-2 U   1-2 U   1-2 U   1-2 U

5b. $\frac{4}{4}$ D   1-2   D   1-2   D   1-2   D   1-2

5c. $\frac{4}{4}$ D   (1)   2   D   -   2   D   -   2   D   -   2

The sixteenth note sounds on the second half of the up beat.

5d. $\frac{4}{4}$ 1   2 (1) 2   1   2   -   2   1   2   -   2   1   2   -   2

The eighth note sounds on the second half of the down beat, and the last sixteenth note sounds on the second half of the up beat.

5e. $\frac{4}{4}$ 1   2   -   1   2   -   1   2   -   1   2   -

The dotted eighth note starts on the second half of the down beat.

6. For notes of more than one beat duration, say the number of beats that the note is to be sustained at the time when note is started.

Example:

$\frac{4}{4}$ 4 downs   3   D   D   2 D 2 D   D 2 D   D   D U 2 D   D

7. This system can be applied to any music which has a 4 for the lower numeral of the meter signature. Set a steady beat and say the symbols as they appear.

Examples:

7a.

7b.

7c.

1. In meter signatures with an 8 underneath and a multiple of three above (3-8, 6-8, 12-8) the dotted quarter note becomes the one or down beat unit at a fast tempo or speed.

Example:

2. The dotted quarter, one beat note, can be divided into three equal eighth notes. After the steady beat is established, count one, two, three on each tap or beat to get the spacing of three equal notes within the beat. It may be helpful to divide the beat into down, middle, and up sections or to think of a three-syllable word (mem-o-ry) to develop the feeling for this division of the beat into three equal parts.

Example:

3. When one of the eighth notes in the pattern is dropped, its number is omitted from the word pattern, or the word "rest" is said in place of the note.

Example:

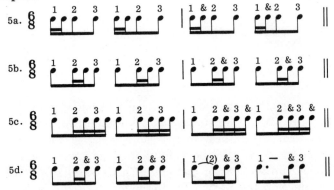

4. The quarter note, eighth note pattern is distinguished from the pattern in paragraph number three by using the word down (D) for the quarter note and three for the eighth note which occurs on the third portion of the beat.

Example:

5. Subdivisions of the basic grouping of three notes to a beat are accomplished by saying the one, two, three pattern and then subdividing when necessary.

Examples:

5a.

5b.

5c.

5d.

Example 5d shows how the dotted eighth figure is developed in 6 - 8 meter.

MANUSCRIPT WRITING

1. When writing melodic lines, notes placed on the middle line of the staff may have stems going upward or downward.

Notice that stems are from two-and-a-half to three spaces wide.

2. Generally when a note is placed above the middle line, the stem comes downward on the left side of the note.

3. When a note is placed below the middle line, the stem goes upward on the right side of the note.

4. a. Flags added to a note are always placed to the right side of the stem.

   b. A succession of flagged notes may be combined into groups for easier reading by the use of beams.

   This calls for an exception to the rule about the direction of stems. Here follow the direction that the greater number of stems take.

5. Dots following a note or rest always should be placed on a space for clarity in reading.

6. Rests are placed in, above, or below the staff in relation to the music context so that they are in the line of vision of the person reading the part.

7. When four mixed voices or parts are used, the two top voices are in treble clef and the stems for the first or soprano part are written upward while the stems for the second or alto part are turned downward. The two lower voices are notated in bass clef and the third or tenor part is written with stems upward while the fourth or bass part is written with stems downward.

8. For information on music writing, refer to:
Harold M. Johnson, *How to Write Music Manuscript*, Carl Fisher Co., New York, 1946.

APPENDIX II

Creating Songs

Songs can be created in many recreational situations. The easiest approach would be to alter the words or text of a familiar song to fit a local circumstance. Another procedure entails writing music for a given poem which may be composed especially for the present occasion or may be taken or adapted from the standard literature. Look for a poem that has a simple, direct, and regular rhythm, for ordinarily the words or text of the poem will dictate the rhythm of the melody with a note for each syllable of the poem.

If the song is to be created by a group, the following procedures are suggested·

1. Write the words for the song on a chalk-board. Leave wide spaces between the lines so that bar lines and rhythmic notation can be added.

2. Have the group say the words in unison to develop a feeling for the rhythm, mood, and meaning of the poetry. Do this several times. Some of the group may wish to respond physically to the rhythm of the verse. When a strong feeling of rhythm has been generated, establish a steady beat as a background for the poetry.

3. Underline the accented syllables in the poem. Accents will occur usually as a part of the important words, the nouns or verbs, that carry the sense or meaning of the text.

4. Determine if the accented syllables fall into groups of two or
   of three, and decide what the meter signature is to be. Once
   the grouping of twos or threes is established, a simple measure
   made up of one of these groupings or a compound measure
   using two or more groupings can be used.
5. Place bar lines for each measure. When working with an
   inexperienced group, it would be advisable to use the general
   rule of a bar line before each accented syllable. If a compound meter is used, there may be two, or three, or four accented
   syllables in each measure.
6. Develop a rhythmic notation above the words of the poem.
   This entails transfer of feeling for accented and unaccented
   syllables into note patterns of long or short duration. The
   kinds of notes used will depend upon the meter signature employed.
7. Compose a melody for the first line or phrase of the poem.
   It is helpful to establish a context of a key, a key center, and
   a regular beat pattern in which to work. In some situations
   an harmonic background of a chord or two in each measure
   can be played to assist in the formation of a melodic line.

$$1. \ \text{I} - \text{I} - \text{V}_7 - \text{I}, \quad \text{I} - \text{I} - \text{V}_7 - \text{I}$$
$$2. \ \text{I} - \text{I} - \text{I} - \text{V}_7, \quad \text{V}_7 - \text{V}_7 - \text{V}_7 - \text{I}$$
$$3. \ \text{I} - \text{IV} - \text{I} - \text{V}_7, \quad \text{I} - \text{IV} - \text{V}_7 - \text{I}$$
$$4. \ \text{I} - \text{IV} - \text{V}_7 - \text{I}, \quad \text{I} - \text{IV} - \text{V}_7 - \text{I}$$

Melodic instruments such as bells, recorders, or piano can be
used to facilitate the development of a melody, but it usually is
better to have individuals try to hear and sing their own ideas
quietly so as not to disturb or influence those around them.

A tape recorder can be utilized to record melodies as they are
developed by individuals; the melodies then can be reviewed, learned
by the group, and the best tune used as a basis for the melody to
follow. This procedure can be repeated several times until the entire
composition is completed.

Where a tape recorder is not available, melodies can be written
on a chalk-board by the leader; they can be developed by the group
by the use of syllables or numbers, or they can be worked out by
letter names at the piano or another fixed-pitch instrument as each
phrase is developed. It is helpful to remember that the melodies will

develop into four, eight, or sixteen measure groupings and will fall into two or four phrases for each stanza.

8. Look and listen in the text for:

   a. *Questions and answers.* Questions suggest a rising and upward tendency in the music which creates a feeling of tension and movement, while the answering sections usually move downward to lower pitches that give a feeling of relaxation and repose.

   b. *Repetitions.* Similar words suggest the use of similar melodies. Repetitions make for unity in a poem or a song; contrasting materials make for variety and heightened interest.

9. If an harmonization was not given as a basis for the development of the melodic line, harmonize the melody that has been composed. One chord to each measure is sufficient in most instances when a simple rhythmic grouping has been used. Use these general rules for harmonization:

   a. When the accented beat of the measure falls on 1, 3, or 5 of the scale, use the I or tonic chord.

   b. When the accented beat of the measure falls on 7 or 2 of the scale, use the V or dominant chord. This may be a dominant triad or a dominant seventh chord.

   c. When the accented beat of the measure falls on 6 or 4 of the scale, use the IV or sub-dominant chord.

APPENDIX III

List of Composers

Albeniz (äl' bā.nēth'), Isaac, b. Camprodon, Spain, 1860-1909

Arensky (a.rĕn' skĕ), Anton, b. Novgorod, Russia, 1861-1906

Bach (bäk), Johann Sebastian, b. Eisenach, Germany, 1685-1750

Bartok (bär' tŏk), Bela, b. Nagyszentmikl'os, Hungary, 1881-1945

Beethoven (bā' tō.vĕn), Ludwig van, b. Bonn, Germany, 1770-1827

Bellini (bĕl.lē' nĕ), Vincenzo, b. Catania, Sicily, 1801-1835

Berlioz (bĕr' lĕ.ōs'), Hector, b. Côte Saint André, France, 1803-1869

Bizet (bē zē'), Georges, b. Paris, France, 1838-1875

Bloch (blŏk), Ernest, b. Geneva, Switzerland, 1880-1959

Boccherini (bŏk' ka.rē' nĕ), Luigi, b. Lucca, Italy, 1743-1805

Borodin (bŏr' ŏ.dĭn'), Alexander, b. St. Petersburg, Russia, 1834-1887

Brahms, (brämz), Johannes, b. Hamburg, Germany, 1833-1897

Bruckner (brook' ner), Anton, b. Ausfelden, Upper Austria, 1824-1896

Byrd (bûrd), William, b. London, England, 1542-1623

Carpenter (kär' pĕn.ter), John Alden b. Park Ridge, Ill., 1876

Chabrier (sha' brē ā), (Alexis) Emanuel, b. Paris, France, 1841-1894

Chadwick (chăd' wĭk), George Whitefield, b. Lowell, Mass., 1854-1931

Chaminade (sha' mē' nad'), Cecile, b. Paris, France, 1861-1944

Charpentier (shar' pan' tyā'), Gustave, b. Dieuze, Lorraine, 1860-1956

Chausson (shô' sôn'), Ernest, b. Paris, France, 1855-1899

Chopin (shô' păn'), Frederic, b. Warsaw, Poland, 1810-1849

Corelli (kō.rĕl' lē), Arcangelo, b. Imola, Italy, 1653-1713

Debussy (de.bü' sē'), Claude Achille, b. Paris, France, 1862-1918

Delibes (de.lēb'), Leo, b. St. Germain-du-Val, France, 1836-1934
Delius (dē' li.us), Frederick, b. Bradford, England, 1863-1934
Dohnanyi (dō' nän'.yě), Ernst von, b. Pressburg, Hungary, 1877
Donizetti (dō' ně.dzět' tě), Gaetano, b. Bergamo, Italy, 1797-1848
Dukas (dü' käh'), Paul, b. Paris, France, 1865-1935
Dvorak (dvor' zhäk), Anton, b. Muhlhausen, Bohemia, 1841-1904
Elgar (el' ger), Edward, b. Worcester, England, 1857-1934
Falla (fäl' yä), Manuel de, b. Cadiz, Spain, 1876-1946
Foster (fos'ter), Stephen Collins, b. Pittsburgh, Pa., 1826-1864
Franck (frångk), Cesar, b. Liege, Belgium, 1822-1890
Gershwin (ger' shwin), George, b. Brooklyn, N. Y., 1898-1937
Gillis (gĭl' is), Don, b. Cameron, Missouri, 1912-
Glazunov (glä zoo.nof'), Alexander, b. St. Petersburg, Russia, 1865-1936
Glinka (glĭng' kä), Michael, b. Smolensk, Russia, 1803-1857
Gluck (glook), Christoph Willibald, von, b. Weidenwang, Upper Pa-
    latinate, 1714-1787
Goldmark (gôlt' mark'), Karl, b. Keszthely, Hungary, 1830-1915
Gounod (goo' nō'), Charles, b. Paris, France, 1818-1893
Grieg (grēg), Edvard, b. Bergen, Norway, 1843-1907
Griffes (grĭf' es), Charles T., b. Elmira, N. Y., 1884-1920
Handel (hăn' d'l), George Frederic, b. Halle, Prussia, 1685-1759
Hanson (hăn' son), Howard, b. Wahoo, Neb., 1896
Haydn (hī' d'n), Franz-Josef, b. Rohrau, Austria, 1732-1809
Hindemith (hin' dě.mĭt), Paul, b. Hanau, Germany, 1895
Holst (hōlst), Gustav, b. Cheltenham, England, 1874-1934
Honegger (hôn' ěg' er), Arthur, b. Le Havre, France, 1892
Humperdinck (hoom' per.dĭngk), Engelbert, b. Bonn, Germany, 1854-
    1921
Indy (ăn dē'), Vincent d', b. Paris, France, 1851-1931
Kodaly (kō.da' ē), Zoltan, b. Kecskemet, Hungary, 1882
Leoncavallo (lā' ôn.kä.väl' lô), Ruggiero, b. Naples, Italy, 1858-1919
Liszt (lĭst), Franz, b. Raiding, Hungary, 1811-1886
Loeffler (lěf' ler), Charles Martin, b. Muhlhausen, Alsace, 1861-1935
MacDowell (măk.dou' ěl), Edward A., b. New York, N.Y., 1861-1908
Mahler (mä' ler), Gustav, b. Kalischt, Bohemia, 1860-1911
Mascagni (mäs.kän' yě), Pietro, b. Leghorn, Italy, 1863-1945
Mason, Lowell, b. Medfield, Mass., 1792-1872
Massenet (mä s' ně'), Jules, b. Montaud, France, 1842-1912
Mendelssohn (měn' děl.sōn), Felix, b. Hamburg, Germany, 1809-1847
Meyerbeer (mī' er.bār), Giacomo, b. Berlin, Germany, 1791-1864
Milhaud (mē' yō'), Darius, b. Aix-en-Provence, France, 1892

Monteverdi (mŏn' tä.var' dĭ), Claudio, b. Cremona, Italy, 1567-1643
Moussorgsky (mōo.sorg' skĕ), Modeste, b. Knrev, Russia, 1839-1881
Mozart (mō' tsärt), Wolfgang Amadeus, b. Salzburg, Austria, 1756-1791
Offenbach (ŏf' ĕn.bäk), Jacques, b. Cologne, Germany, 1819-1880
Paganini (pä' gä.nē' nĕ), Niccolo, b. Genoa, Italy, 1782-1840
Palestrina (pä' läs.trē' nä), Giovanni Pierluigi da, b. Palestrina near Rome, Italy, 1525-1594
Prokofiev (prō.kō' fē.ĕf), Serge, b. Sontzovka, Russia, 1891-1953
Puccini (poot.chē' nĕ), Giacomo, b. Lucca, Italy, 1858-1924
Purcell (pur' sĕl), Henry, b. London, England, 1658-1695
Rachmaninoff (räk.mä' nĕ.nŏf), Sergei, b. Onega, Russia, 1874-1943
Ravel (rà vĕl'), Maurice, b. Ciboure, France, 1875-1937
Respighi (rĕs.pē' gĕ), Ottorino, b. Bologna, Italy, 1879-1936
Rimsky-Korsakoff (rĭm' skĕ-kor' sà.kŏf), Nicholas, b. Novgorod, Russia, 1844-1908
Rossini (rŏs.sē' nĕ), Gioacchino, b. Pesaro, Italy, 1792-1868
Saint-Saens (săn' säns'), Charles Camille, b. Paris, France, 1834-1921
Schoenberg (shun' bĕrk), Arnold, b. Vienna, Austria, 1874-1952
Schubert (shoo' bĕrt), Franz, b. Vienna, Austria, 1797-1828
Schumann (shoo' män), Robert, b. Zwickau, Saxony, 1810-1856
Shostakovich (shŏs.tä.kō' vĭch), Dmitri, b. Leningrad, Russia, 1906
Sibelius (sĭ.bä' lĭ.oos), Jean, b. Tavastehus, Finland, 1865-1957
Smetana (smĕ' tä.nä), Bedrich, b. Leitomischl, Bohemia, 1824-1884
Strauss (shtrous), Johann, Jr., b. Vienna, Austria, 1825-1899
Strauss (shtrous), Richard, b. Munich, Germany, 1864-1949
Stravinsky (stra.vĭn' skĕ), Igor, b. near Petrograd, Russia, 1882
Taylor (tā' ler), Deems, b. New York, N. Y., 1885
Tschaikovsкy (chī.kŏf' skĕ), Peter Ilich, b Votkinsk, Russia, 1840-1893
Thomas (tŏ mä'), Ambroise, b. Metz, France, 1811-1896
Vaughan Williams (von wĭl' yämz), Ralph, b. Wiltshire, England, 1872-1958
Verdi (var' dĕ), Giuseppe, b. Le Roncole, Parma, Italy, 1813-1901
Wagner (väg' ner), Richard, b. Leipzig, Germany, 1813-1883
Weber (vä' ber), Carl Maria von, b. Oldenburg, Germany, 1786-1826

Professional Organizations in Recreation and Music

AMERICAN MUSIC CONFERENCE
332 South Michigan Blvd., Chicago 4, Illinois

A noncommercial and nonprofit organization supported by the music industry, it seeks to encourage music education in schools; to increase appreciation for music in the home and church; to sponsor recreational and avocational activities in music; and to foster the growth and development of community musical participation.

COOPERATIVE RECREATION SERVICE, INC.
Radnor Road, Delaware, Ohio

This service "grew out of the interest of people in making their own good times." It features tested materials for group parties, game making, folk dancing, and singing. Over 2,000 songs from all over the world are available in inexpensive, paper-bound books.

MUSIC EDUCATORS NATIONAL CONFERENCE
1201 16th St., N. W., Washington, D. C.

An organization of music educators who are interested in the promotion, recognition, and acceptance of a balanced program of music in schools. The Conference publishes the MUSIC EDUCATORS JOURNAL and the JOURNAL OF RESEARCH IN MUSIC EDUCATION.

MUSIC TEACHERS NATIONAL ASSOCIATION
775 Brooklyn Ave., Baldwin, N. Y.

This association publishes the AMERICAN MUSIC TEACHER and works to raise the professional, musical, and financial status of music teachers in the United States.

NATIONAL ASSOCIATION FOR MUSIC THERAPY
c/o Ervin H. Schneider, Dept. of Music Education, University of of Tennessee, Knoxville, Tennessee

The BULLETIN OF THE NATIONAL ASSOCIATION FOR MUSIC THERAPY is the official publication of this group which works for standardization of training, certification, and registration of music therapists.

NATIONAL RECREATION ASSOCIATION
8 West 8th Street, New York 11, N. Y.

The National Recreation Association is the professional association for recreation workers. Its official publication is RECREATION, a valuable source of splendid materials in all branches of recreational activities.

Index

SONG INDEX

211

CLASSIFIED SONG INDEX

ACTIVITY SONGS

CHANTS AND DESCANTS

COMBINED SONGS

FAREWELL SONGS

FOREIGN SONGS